Raising Readers at Home

Raising Readers at Home

An Easy-to-Follow Plan to Implement a Foundation for Reading in the Home

Sheila E. Sapp

ROWMAN & LITTLEFIELD
Lanham • Boulder • New York • London

Published by Rowman & Littlefield
An imprint of The Rowman & Littlefield Publishing Group, Inc.
4501 Forbes Boulevard, Suite 200, Lanham, Maryland 20706
www.rowman.com

86-90 Paul Street, London EC2A 4NE

British Library Cataloguing in Publication Information Available

Library of Congress Cataloging-in-Publication Data

Names: Sapp, Sheila E., author.
Title: Raising readers at home : an easy-to-follow plan to implement a foundation for reading in the home / Sheila E. Sapp.
Description: Lanham, Maryland : Rowman & Littlefield, 2023. | Includes bibliographical references.
Identifiers: LCCN 2023017198 (print) | LCCN 2023017199 (ebook) | ISBN 9781475869699 (cloth) | ISBN 9781475869705 (paperback) | ISBN 9781475869712 (ebook)
Subjects: LCSH: Reading—Parent participation. | Reading readiness. | Reading (Early childhood)
Classification: LCC LB1050.2 .S27 2023 (print) | LCC LB1050.2 (ebook) | DDC 372.41/4—dc23/eng/20230510
LC record available at https://lccn.loc.gov/2023017198
LC ebook record available at https://lccn.loc.gov/2023017199

♾™ The paper used in this publication meets the minimum requirements of American National Standard for Information Sciences—Permanence of Paper for Printed Library Materials, ANSI/NISO Z39.48-1992.

This book is dedicated to all parents and caregivers who are
their children's first teachers. It is indeed an honor to
write a resource handbook to help parents/caregivers nurture,
raise, and produce successful future readers at home.
Also, I want to thank my husband, Everette, and daughter,
Nicholyn, for their continued support and assistance with my endeavors.

Children are made readers in the laps of their parents.

—Emilie Buchwald

Contents

Preface

Schools continue to face the challenge of increasing reading achievement and need parents and caregivers to assist them with this endeavor. Researchers have proven the importance of parental involvement and its positive impact on increasing academic achievement scores. Parents and caregivers can play a vital role in their child's reading journey by fostering a love for reading and laying a solid foundation for learning to read in a familiar environment. The purpose of this resource book is to provide parents and caregivers with a plan consisting of prereading literacy skills that can be nurtured, implemented, and supported in the home.

Parents and caregivers who are familiar with their children's developmental milestones and preliteracy or prereading skills can support the learning-to-read process. With additional support and instruction from parents/caregivers, children can gain confidence and experience success while embarking on their reading journey. This reading plan is designed to equip and help parents and caregivers provide specific activities, games, and exercises to implement at home to ensure their children's obtainment of prereading skills needed for learning to read.

The easy-to-follow raising readers plan begins with a brief discussion about reasons why children may struggle with learning to read. Parents and caregivers are exposed to developmental milestones and stages and behavior characteristics that are signs of emerging prereading skills. Also, included is a self-assessment instrument to assist parents and caregivers in determining their beliefs, values, and principles about learning. All parents and caregivers are their children's *first* teachers and need to know who they are themselves as learners. Knowing who they are as learners will help parents and caregivers create positive and vibrant learning environments for their children.

Each major component of reading is addressed in chapters 3, 4, and 5. They are knowledge of letter names and sounds (visual and auditory discrimination of letters), phonemic awareness, auditory discrimination (letter sounds), auditory blending of letters, consonant clusters, vowels, digraphs, and building and using sight words. In chapter 7, word families are added as a special feature to extend and enhance a child's vocabulary development. Parents and caregivers are recommended to first determine their child's motivation and interest in learning additional words before starting chapter 7. This chapter is for children who are five or six years old.

Parents and caregivers are encouraged to spend extended time as needed to ensure their children obtain a working knowledge and understanding of the three main layers of the reading-at-home plan (chapters 3, 4, and 5). All activities consist of instructions, materials needed, and implementation directions. Also, templates and patterns and alternative options are incorporated to give parents and caregivers visual and verbal examples to follow. Additionally, readers may use the book as a workbook for their instruction. The additional alternate activities and exercises provided enable parents and caregivers to address specific learning needs and developmental levels.

Although the focus of this reading plan is on early learners ages two to six years old, children who are developmentally delayed or diagnosed with selected special needs would benefit from selected exercises, games, and activities provided. Additionally, this plan was designed for ease of implementation by other significant members of the household or older siblings. Users of this resource book do not need a degree in reading to implement and perform the instructional lessons. Parents and caregivers are not required to be avid readers themselves to raise readers at home. It does, however, require support, commitment, and consistency.

Parents and caregivers and other significant members in the home working as a team can help make the learning-to-read process smooth and adventurous for children. In a world filled with technology, devices, videos, and educational apps, there is no substitute for parent-child interactions and communication. Children will continue to receive their information and knowledge from printed material (textbooks). Therefore, becoming a proficient reader is critical and fundamental for all children.

Introduction

We live in a world in which literacy is a necessity for life. Reading, one of four basic literacy skills, is an important skill all children need to acquire and master. When children do not learn to read, their general knowledge, writing, spelling, vocabulary development, and comprehension suffer too. They spend from kindergarten through second grade in elementary school learning the mechanics of reading. In grades third through fifth, however, the emphasis shifts from mastering the mechanics of reading to reading to gain knowledge and information. The expectation is that children should be proficient and skilled readers by the end of third grade.

Not all children, however, are proficient and skilled in reading by the end of second grade. They have not mastered the basic mechanics of reading and begin to fall behind their peers who aren't experiencing reading difficulties. Not only are they falling behind in reading, but they also have trouble acquiring knowledge and information in other core subjects such as mathematics, science, and social studies. Their lack of reading sufficiency eventually impacts their self-confidence and self-esteem throughout their academic journey from elementary school up through high school and beyond.

Although schools are fighting to improve overall reading achievement and to close reading gaps, children who begin their educational journey behind in kindergarten never *catch up*. The consequences of this struggle to catch up students, who are behind academically, pose far-reaching consequences. Students who start kindergarten behind form the largest group of high school dropouts. Also, there is less than a 12 percent chance to attend an institution of higher learning. Additionally, there is a connection between illiteracy and crime. Over 70 percent of inmates in America's prisons cannot read above the fourth-grade level. Other statistics about low literacy and incarceration are:

1

- Eighty-five percent of all juveniles who interface with the juvenile court system are functionally literate.
- Juvenile incarceration reduces the probability of high school graduation and increases the probability of incarceration later in life.
- Students who drop out of high school are five times more likely than high school graduates to be arrested during their lifetime.
- Students who drop out of high school are 63 percent more likely to be incarcerated than their peers with four-year college degrees.

The rigors of schooling, homework, and increasing text complexity compound the lack of reading proficiency among struggling students. Reading serves as a major foundational skill for all school and home-based learning. Without the skill of reading, students' chances for academic and occupational success are limited. Also, reading achievement gaps that develop among and between students in elementary school persist and are even wider by their high school years.

Despite supplemental state and federally funded remedial reading programs providing additional support, below-grade-level readers still exist. In a year, they must make up past years' growth plus the current year's growth expectation. This creates, for struggling readers, a challenge that is almost impossible to achieve for the below average student. Also, this becomes an impossibility for students who are special needs with additional specific disabilities that impact their ability to learn. Should parents and caregivers be proficient readers themselves to nurture and develop a love for reading in their children?

Additionally, are there prereading skills that help lay the foundation for learning how to read and the reading process itself? What role can parents and caregivers play in helping schools close gaps and improve overall reading achievement on state and national assessments? Researchers have emphasized the positive effect and impact parents' and caregivers' involvement has on children's educational achievement, growth, and behavior. There is a need to start the process of preparing children for their literacy journey and laying the foundation for reading earlier.

Gaps in reading proficiency and struggles to learn to read begin before children start school or receive formal instruction. Children are still entering preschool or kindergarten without any exposure to letters, print, and language. Parents and caregivers who don't support or provide activities to nurture the development of preliteracy skills in their children are compacting and increasing nonproficient readers. The early years of children's development are critical to establishing a foundation for preliteracy skills before formal reading instruction. Learning to read is a challenge for all children whether they are in school or homeschooled.

What are preliteracy skills and why are they important for the process of learning to read? Also, when should parents and caregivers introduce their child and children to reading? What preliteracy skills are related to reading? There are basic preliteracy skills that all children need as they progress throughout school. Following is a list of preliteracy skills with a brief explanation for your review and understanding.

- Visual Memory: The ability to remember what has been seen. This is important for learning sight words, letter formations, and combinations of letters.
- Visual Discrimination: The ability to see and tell differences and similarities in letters and words (b, d; bad, dad).
- Auditory Discrimination: The ability to hear the differences and similarities in sounds and words.
- Retelling a Story: To be able to retell a story after being read to or told a story.
- Predicting Sequence: To be able to guess or predict what will happen next and the sequence of events.
- Cause and Effect: To know why something happens and what action led to the consequence of the action.
- Picture Reading: To be able to read a story and understand what's happening by looking at the picture. Included also is being able to answer questions about the story by only the use of the picture.
- Visual Literacy: The ability to understand and make meaning of the information in the form of an image.
- Matching: The ability to find pictures or concepts that are like one another.
- Focusing on Detail: The ability to focus on smaller and less obvious details.
- Sound Awareness: The ability to hear and interpret sounds. This includes listening for sounds, identifying sounds, telling sounds apart, and more.
- Rhyme Awareness: The ability to recognize that sounds and words rhyme.
- Letter Knowledge: The ability to recognize letters and their formation through exposure and physical play with letters.
- Name Recognition: The ability to recognize the letters in their name and *read* their name on a sheet of paper.
- Pattern Recognition: The ability to see and recognize a pattern. They see shapes and patterns and recognize the relationship between them and predict the missing piece in a pattern.

- Phonological Awareness: The ability to hear specific sounds within words. This includes hearing sounds, breaking up sounds, and putting them back together again.
- Spatial Orientation: The child's understanding of how his or her body functions in space. When they learn to orientate themselves, they can later learn and apply this skill to reading and writing, such as moving their eyes from left to right on a page and spacing letters on a page.

Other questions addressed in this plan are:

- When should parents and caregivers introduce their children to reading?
- How do you determine when a child is ready for prereading instruction and activities at home?
- How can parents and caregivers nurture, develop, raise, and lay a solid foundation for future readers?
- What are the signs and behaviors exhibited by children who are developing prereading skills?

The author will discuss and explore these questions throughout this implementation guide and plan. The purpose of this resource book is to provide parents and caregivers with a plan to help prepare their children to learn to read. Children who have mastered prereading skills before formal schooling or homeschooling struggle less with learning how to read. They also are more likely to become proficient readers at home and in school. Progress during the learning-to-read journey flows well when not blocked or hindered by weak or nonexistent necessary prereading skills. Therefore, parents and caregivers need to ensure they are providing appropriate experiences at home to promote and support reading.

Although there is a plethora of prereading skills as mentioned earlier, the author chose to focus on visual recognition and discrimination of letters, phonemic awareness, auditory discrimination, auditory blending (letter, consonants, and vowels), sight words, word families, and comprehension (listening and reading). This plan is recommended for children ages two to five years old. There are, however, children who may exhibit prereading behaviors earlier or later. The plan consists of suggested and recommended start times, but it is each child's individual developmental stage and intellectual growth that should guide his or her journey.

Additionally, the activities and games utilized will incorporate many of the other preliteracy skills listed. The activities included in the plan encourages physical movement and active engagement. Parents and caregivers need to continually observe and watch for signs and behaviors as children move through the different stages of their developmental and intellectual growth. It is their responsibility to support and encourage children with appropriate experiences, exposures, activities, and positive engagements to foster the love of reading and learning.

The raising readers at home plan presented in this resource book consists of different instructional activities, techniques, and games centered on the basic components of reading-phonemic awareness, letter and sound recognition, vocabulary development, fluency, and comprehension. Also, the activities and games are designed to be easy and simple to follow with clear instructions, directions, and implementation for home use. Written *scripts* (selected lessons only) serve as a guide for the readers to follow while conducting the lessons. Additionally, parents and caregivers are encouraged to review and maintain prereading skills learned.

Another important feature is the resource book's flexibility and format. Readers and users will be able to individualize the plan to fit their child's specific prereading skill needs. Parents and caregivers can select the reading component that addresses the area needed by their child and children. By doing so, readers determine and select activities, games, and instructional techniques that align with their child's individual prereading readiness and developmental levels. The author has selected games and activities that incorporate items in the home or are low cost to purchase if materials are needed for the activity and lesson.

To assist parents and caregivers with selecting activities and games and determine where their children are developmentally in the plan, a checklist, a list of prereading skill behaviors, and examples of behaviors to look for are included in the resource book. These tools help parents and caregivers gauge which stage and developmental level their children are currently in while implementing the raising readers plan. Parents' and caregivers' increased knowledge about their children's prereading skill level abilities enables them to provide proper support needed to foster and develop prereading skills in children.

The activities and lessons promote and encourage parent and caregiver direct involvement and participation in laying the foundation for reading. Each chapter concludes with a summary of the key highlights of each reading component presented and discussed by the author. Also, optional supplemental practice activities to extend the learning experiences of children needing additional exposure are added as an additional unique feature for developmental delays or enrichment needs. Additionally, the activities presented can serve as a springboard for parents and caregivers to create and design their activities and games.

Parents and caregivers are an integral and essential part of this plan. The author commends you for accepting this opportunity and journey to help ensure a positive reading experience for your child and children. As you utilize and follow this plan designed to develop future successful readers, remember children develop and grow at different rates. They also may acquire or master preliteracy reading skills during different stages and ages. Being familiar with every aspect of your child's growth and development enables you to meet his or her needs. Seek appropriate professional help if your child is experiencing long delays and difficulties during the learning-to-read process.

Finally, parents and caregivers should view their home as a *living* learning laboratory. Every room and household activity performed in your home provides learning experiences that foster a love for reading and learning. Every parent and caregiver is their child's *first* teacher. You can *raise* readers as well as future contributors and members of our society.

Chapter One

Why Johnnie and Suzie Can't Read

The process of learning to read involves mastering selected prereading skills before formal instruction in school or homeschooling. Some children struggle to acquire the skill of reading. Although learning to read is a process that requires proficiency in several skills, some children are ready to read or are reading before formal instruction. Why do children have difficulty learning to read? What are the factors or causes that impede the ability to learn how to read? Are there early signs during a child's developmental growth that serve as a predictor of challenges for reading?

According to Cutting (2017), an early predictor for having difficulty with learning to read may be the result of a family's history. If parents or relatives struggled to learn to read as children, a propensity to have reading problems may be inherited from upcoming family members or siblings. Children born in a family with a history of reading difficulties are genetically at risk. Reading has a biological component that is an early predictor of the ability to learn to read. Knowing the root causes of nonreaders and factors putting children at risk for reading problems justifies early identification and appropriate remediation programs.

Environmental factors such as a child's home, school, social, and culture influence the acquisition of reading. Children in poverty and children with limited English proficiency often suffer from a lack of exposure to learning experiences, vocabulary, and language development. They enter pre-K and kindergarten behind their peers who have had a wealth of stimulating learning experiences, rich vocabularies, and strong language development. Their counterparts are better prepared and ready for formal instruction. These children have an established connection with the print world around them. They know the relationship between what is spoken and read.

Also, other factors (physical) that may impede and impact the ability to learn to read are visual and hearing impairments, dyslexia (difficulty in learning to read and interpret words, letters, and other symbols), slow processing, and attention deficit disorders. Parents and caregivers who suspect any of those factors should seek advice and professional assistance. Early identification of specific reading problems enables the implementation of focused intervention and remediation strategies by appropriate service providers or specially trained school personnel.

Additionally, there are beginning reading (preliteracy) skills that parents and caregivers can nurture and develop during their children's early learning years. These early literacy skills are vital and critical to the reading process. The act of reading involves and requires other skills and abilities such as eye-hand coordination, being able to hold a book and turn the pages, understanding a story, and learning basic sight words. Children who have mastered beginning reading skills or preliteracy skills early begin the reading process with more success and ease. They have learned and understand that the letters on a page are words that have meaning.

Currently, schools (public and private) are working diligently to close achievement gaps in reading and other areas. Federal and state monies fund special reading programs to provide remedial education and intervention for underachieving reading students. The gaps, however, among and between students and subgroups still exist. Schools cannot close reading gaps without the support and assistance of parents and caregivers. Researchers have studied and found the positive impact and effect parents' and caregivers' involvement has on their children's overall academic achievement and well-being.

Improving reading performances does not happen overnight. Schools and parents and caregivers need to work together to decrease reading achievement gaps and produce more proficient readers. Collaboration between home and school will help improve reading achievement and decrease reading performance gaps. Laying a foundation for learning to read begins before a child's birth and continues during the early childhood years. The foundation for reading should consist of appropriate early stimulating experiences with language and reading. Parents and caregivers can nurture, encourage a love for reading, and raise readers at home.

To become successful readers, a variety of different skills or components need to come together for children. Reading consists of phonemic awareness, letter and sound recognition, vocabulary development, fluency, and comprehension. Children who are lacking or are weak in any of the reading components are at risk. They will experience a difficult reading journey that will impact them through adulthood. How can parents and caregivers prepare their children for reading? Can they determine if their child is ready to develop prereading literacy skills? Are there developmental signs that indicate a child's readiness for prereading activities at home?

Researchers have proven that babies (in utero) benefit from listening to stories read aloud. Babies begin hearing sounds around eighteen weeks into pregnancy. After eighteen weeks, their hearing develops rapidly which enables them to distinguish voices. Parents who talk and read stories aloud to their babies form a bond before their children are born. Reading aloud to babies and toddlers also allows them to develop language skills. They become familiar with the language heard although they don't understand the meaning of the language read. Exposing children to books early encourages positive memories of reading and promotes a love for reading.

It is a known fact that parents and caregivers are their children's *first teachers*. Everything a child learns and experiences comes from significant family members and the home environment. Parents and caregivers have the perfect opportunity to nurture and prepare children for reading when young children are open to absorbing everything in their immediate environment. It is during children's early formative years that parents and caregivers lay a foundation for a child's life. Given the appropriate stimulating experiences and exposures, children can obtain prereading skills to help ensure a more positive experience during the process of learning to read.

The key for parents and caregivers is knowing when their child is ready developmentally to acquire prereading skills. Children mature at different rates developmentally as well as intellectually. Parents and caregivers need to be very observant and familiar with their child's emotional, physical, and intellectual growth. There are reading developmental milestones to help parents and caregivers determine what developmental stage their child and children are in. This knowledge and information will assist them in providing the proper experiences, activities, and resources to encourage the development of preliteracy reading skills at home.

It is important to note and remind parents and caregivers, however, that children develop at different paces and spend different amounts of time in each of the stages. The reading milestones presented in this resource guide are from infancy through second grade. Parents and caregivers need to share any concerns about their child not showing or demonstrating the age milestones noted to the child's doctor, teacher, or reading specialist (public and private). The reading milestones will serve as a guide and resource to assist in creating environments for reading success.

According to Zettler-Greely (2018), reading milestones occur during children's early developmental stages. Parents and caregivers can use the reading milestones preliteracy behaviors to implement appropriate activities at home. The reading milestones are as follows:

Babies (Up to Age One)

Babies usually begin to:

- learn that gestures and sounds communicate meaning
- respond when spoken to
- direct their attention to a person or object
- understand fifty words or more
- reach for books and turn the pages with help
- respond to stories and pictures by vocalizing and patting the pictures

Toddlers (Ages One to Three)

Toddlers usually begin to:

- answer questions about and identify objects in books
- name familiar pictures
- point to identified named objects
- pretend to read books
- finish sentences in books they know well
- scribble on paper
- know the names of books and identify them by the picture on the cover
- turn the pages of board books
- have a favorite book and request the book to be read often

Early Preschool (Age Three)

Three-year-olds usually begin to:

- explore books indecently
- listen to longer books that are read aloud
- retell a familiar story
- sing the alphabet song with prompting and cues

Late Preschool (Age Four)

Four-year-olds usually begin to:

- recognize familiar signs and labels, especially on signs and containers
- recognize words that rhyme
- name some of the letters of the alphabet (strive for a goal of fifteen to eighteen uppercase letters)

- recognize the letters in their names
- print their name
- name beginning letters or sounds of words
- match some of the letters to their sounds
- develop an awareness of syllables
- use familiar letters to try to write words
- understand that print is read from left to right, top to bottom
- retell stories that have been read to them

Kindergarten (Age Five)

Five-year-olds usually begin to:

- produce words that rhyme
- match some spoken and written words
- write some letters, numbers, and words
- recognize some familiar words in print
- predict what will happen next in a story
- identify and manipulate increasingly smaller sounds in speech
- understand concrete definitions of some words
- read simple words in isolation (the word in with definition) and in context (using the word in a sentence)
- retell the main idea, identify details (who, what when, where, why, how), and arrange story events in sequence

First and Second Grade (Ages Six to Seven)

Six- and seven-year-olds usually begin to:

- read familiar stories
- "sound out" or decode unfamiliar words
- use pictures and context to figure out unfamiliar words
- use some common punctuation and capitalization in writing
- self-correct when they make a mistake while reading aloud
- show comprehension of a story through drawings
- write by organizing details into a logical sequence with a beginning, middle, and end

The lives of parents and caregivers with babies, toddlers, and preschool-age children can be hectic. Childrearing along with managing and running a household doesn't always provide enough quality time needed to promote prereading skills in the home. Being aware and knowing those reading milestones helps parents and caregivers select and implement activities to ensure an easier transition for their children learning to read. The reading milestones information along with the outlined plan serves as a viable resource to assist parents and caregivers in raising readers at home.

Learning to read is one of the most challenging tasks children will encounter. Reading is a skill that affects all future learning and information children gain for the rest of their lives. Individuals who struggle with reading or never become proficient readers limit their future livelihood and overall well-being. Parents and caregivers who want to play a viable role in laying a foundation for their children's reading success begin their children's reading journey during early childhood. A college education or reading specialist degree is not needed to help children acquire prereading skills at home before utilizing formal instructional strategies.

What is needed, however, is a commitment to using and implementing all aspects of the planned activities designed to help nurture and develop prereading skills for each of the major components of reading. Also, all members of the household must support the plan and participate willingly. The home becomes an active and vibrant learning lab full of stimulating reading-related experiences and activities. Everyone in the home environment has an important part in the formation of the reading foundation of children.

The fact that you are reading this book indicates your interest and commitment to being a vital and involved part of your children's reading journey. Before you begin assess how you feel about reading and your commitment toward the process of learning to read. Below are questions for your consideration and reflection. Share these questions with your spouse and other key significant individuals in the household. Developing prereading skills or preliteracy is a team effort. Everyone in the household should support the process. All experiences and exposures must promote and encourage the formation of prereading skills for young children.

Commitment to Prereading Skills Development Reflection Questions

- Am I willing to support learning at home?
- Am I willing to set aside quality time (ten to fifteen minutes) to read aloud to my child daily?
- Am I willing to provide experiences and activities to encourage reading in my home?
- Am I willing to expose my child to the print world inside and outside my home?

- Am I willing to use the rooms in my home as learning stations?
- Am I willing to use everyday household activities to promote reading?
- Am I willing to provide access to books and other forms of print?
- Am I willing to enlist the assistance of others in my household to develop prereading skills?
- Am I willing to observe my child as he or she progresses through the reading milestone?
- Am I willing to seek professional assistance if any developmental issues arise?

These questions serve as an excellent way to encourage discussion and self-reflection within the household. The reflection questions are included to generate discussions and conversations among key individuals in the home. Complete buy-in and active participation by all members of the family ensures successful implementation of the plan designed to raise readers. Additionally, if the family works as a team, they'll be able to utilize each other's strengths to meet the specific needs of the children in the home.

CHAPTER 1 SUMMARY

Learning to read is the most vital skill children will face entering school or homeschooling. Reading is a skill that paves the way for the acquisition of knowledge and understanding throughout an individual's lifetime. Reading is vital, complex, and necessary for the livelihood of everyone. The author shared and discussed factors that may affect and impact one's ability to learn how to read. Schools are still facing the challenge of closing reading performance gaps between and among students. The gaps begin in elementary school and increase through high school.

Research has shown how parents' and caregivers' involvement with their children's education can have a positive effect on academic growth and achievement. With the assistance of parents and caregivers, schools (public, private, and in the home) can help reduce the number of nonproficient readers. Additionally, early recognition and intervention of reading difficulties enable the utilization of appropriate remedial strategies, techniques, and programs. Parents and caregivers play a key and integral role in nurturing a foundation for reading during children's early years.

Despite differing opinions about how early learning to read should begin, children who enter school and homeschool with prereading or preliteracy skills have an easier time acquiring the ability to learn how to read. Babies and toddlers benefit from being read aloud during their early years. Exposure to reading at an early age introduces language and promotes a love for reading. Babies' hearing is developed in utero at eighteen weeks which enables them to recognize their parents' and caregivers' voices after birth. Additionally, parents and caregivers strengthen the bond with their children as well as foster a love for reading at an early age.

As children grow and develop during their early years, there are age-related stages of reading milestones that children experience developmentally. These reading milestones provide a road map of skills that parents and caregivers can use to assess and determine their children's readiness for prereading or preliteracy skills. Utilization of this information enables parents and caregivers to provide appropriate activities and strategies to prepare children for learning to read successfully. Parents and caregivers need to remember that children have different maturation and developmental levels.

Therefore, children may acquire outlined reading milestones earlier or later than noted. Extended developmental delays and observed severe difficulties should be referred to a doctor or professional for assistance. Early identification and intervention allow for the implementation of appropriate strategies to make learning to read a possibility for children experiencing difficulties. Children who are lagging in learning to read become better readers when techniques and strategies are used that are designed to strengthen their specific deficit reading component area.

Chapter 2 will share the first steps in preparing the home for nurturing reading by developing a home environment before children are ready to read. These first steps are critical for laying a foundation to raise readers at home. The steps needed to begin the process of building a solid foundation for reading are you and the established home environment. Let's see what factors should be considered as the footing or first layer for the foundation.

Chapter Two

Setting the Stage

Before They Are Ready to Read

The big day has finally arrived! You have planned and prepared for your new son's or daughter's arrival for nine months. Now, you get to take him or her home at last. You have checked everything off on your list and you are ready to begin this new journey. The room is decorated and prepared for its new occupant. The room is equipped to accommodate the baby as he or she grows and develops. A mobile is placed over the top of the crib for the child to view. Pictures, their name, and alphabet letters are on the wall. There's a shelf in a corner or a small cubby filled with books for reading aloud. The stage is set, but are the key role models ready?

Being a parent and caregiver is not an easy task. It is much easier to decorate and plan and set up a room for a new baby than to set the stage and know how to prepare a home for optimal learning from birth to the time formal instruction begins at school or homeschooling. How can parents and caregivers begin the process of preparing themselves? Since parents and caregivers play a vital role in childrearing and are their children's *first* teachers, the following are selected excerpts of questions to discuss, think about, and reflect on their reactions for preparation and planning.

EXCERPTS FROM CREATING AN ENVIRONMENT TO FOSTER LEARNING; SELF-ASSESSMENT

- How do I learn best or what is my preference (kinesthetic, visual, auditory, or, tactile)?
- What is my temperament?
- How do I approach challenges?
- Do I always see the glass as half empty or half full?

- Do I believe you can learn from mistakes?
- Do I value education?
- Am I patient and tolerant?
- Am I a lifelong learner?
- How do I view failure?
- Am I open to new and different ideas?
- Am I open to constructive criticism?
- Am I supportive?
- Am I curious?
- Do I have high expectations?
- Am I interested in learning?
- Do I provide a variety of meaningful educational experiences for my child and children?
- Am I resourceful and creative?
- Do I support learning at home? If so, how?
- Am I currently involved with my child's learning?

The author recommends parents and caregivers follow up their reflections and thoughts with honest and open dialogue with all significant individuals in the home. A unity of purpose and teamwork will develop in the household that ensures success for all. With a united and dedicated team in the home, children will be able to tackle any experiences or challenges they may face. Starting with parents' and caregivers' personal beliefs and feeling about learning is an important first step in setting the stage for learning. Another aspect is looking at the factors that impact learning in the home. Which factors can nurture brain development and learning at home?

LEARNING AND THE HOME ENVIRONMENT

Setting the stage for early learning and prereading skills in the home is critical for the intellectual and developmental growth of children. According to Mcilroy (2023), the overall brain development of children needs a stimulating learning environment. Reading as well as other areas of learning in the future are impacted by what happens within the immediate surroundings of young children starting at birth. It is a known fact that children must have basic needs such as food, shelter, security, and love. Learning cannot take place until basic needs are met. There are, however, other home environmental factors to consider in nurturing and encouraging learning.

Environmental factors that impact children are the physical environment in which they live, the physical things around them, the people around them, and the interactions they have with people and the world. Focusing on these environmental factors will assist you in preparing your home. You may want to ask yourself and others in your household how they can contribute to the physical aspect of the home environment. In what ways can they support a child's learning by their behaviors and actions? Does their presence surround the child with peace, love, calmness, and a sense of security?

Parents and caregivers need to be an anchor for their children as a part of the early learning process. Babies thrive when their physical and emotional needs are met. Children who experience love, care, and acceptance are prepared psychologically to explore their surrounding environment without fear and trepidation. They are naturally curious about everything that appears in their world. Also, parents and caregivers can promote learning and the motivation to learn by being available, supportive, and present for their children. Without emotional support, children's natural curiosity, excitement, and exploration of the world around them are blocked.

Children who feel unloved and insecure are timid and reluctant to experience the environment on their own. Additionally, they are hesitant about interacting with others outside of their immediate family circle. They are content to be passively involved with others outside of their home environment. Also, children's interaction and involvement with learning become closed and marginal. They have little or no desire to extend their learning and experiences by reaching out to the unknown and unpredictable. Unmet physical and emotional needs will affect the process of producing and laying a solid foundation needed to nurture a learner and reader.

After meeting the physical and emotional needs of children, parents and caregivers are now ready to focus on other aspects of the home environment. According to Mcilroy (2022), once the home is set up for learning children can be successful in learning and obtaining skills at home. Now, it is time to explore other items that will assist in stimulating and encouraging learning. The process of learning to read is complex and begins when children are young. Reading, not like learning to speak, is a process that must be taught. Below are suggested tips and activities for you to consider doing and using to support the reading process in your home.

- *Give your child and children access to books.* Expose your child and children to a variety of books to create a reading environment at home: picture books, fiction, nonfiction, and reference books like *Pictionary for Children*. Visit the library to check out books and participate in storytelling activities offered. Also, children who see their parents or caregivers reading books view reading as an enjoyable activity and develop a love for reading.

- *Provide rich sensory experiences.* From birth through their early years, children learn through their seven senses: touch, taste, smell, sight, hearing, balance, and body awareness. Parents' and caregivers' homes should provide continuous experiences to smell, taste new things, see, and hear various sounds, and develop their tactile senses. Additionally, children should be moving nonstop to develop a sense of balance and body awareness. Activities such as playing with puzzles, playing matching games, singing, listening to music, participating in listening games, baking, reciting rhymes, gardening, and moving—rolling, jumping, hopping, twirling, and crawling through tunnels.
- *Create functional spaces for different activities in the home.* Children tend to use areas set aside for specific different activities such as reading (a corner with books), drawing, painting, or molding clay (a small table or easel), and writing (a small desk or table). Outdoors is a great place for movement, sand and water play, science experiments, running, blocks for building, and nature walks.
- *Provide educational toys.* Educational toys are good tools for stimulating learning and sensory experiences. Maintain a healthy balance between toys that flash and ring and *old-fashioned* toys such as puzzles, wooden blocks, threading and lacing boards, matching games, construction toys, board games, balls, and bean bags. Electronic devices help develop skills, but they are limited in the amount of creativity fostered. Saved refrigerator boxes and other large appliance cardboard boxes can become forts and make-believe houses or campers.

Parents and caregivers can use different rooms in their homes to set up functional stations for learning. Rooms such as a kitchen, bedroom, and family room, and backyard are natural areas to support and foster learning. Following is a list of selected examples of simple activities you can do to provide sensory experiences at home. Note the list is not all-inclusive and is provided to increase awareness of what is readily available in homes.

What's cooking? Let your child guess what is for dinner through their sense of smell.

No peeking! Tell your child to close his or her eyes and tell you what they smell.

Baking Experiences. An activity all children will enjoy is licking the bowl after you have poured the cake or pie mix batter out of the bowl. Instruct them to tell you how it tastes to them. Is it sweet? Does it taste like chocolate or strawberry? Compare the taste of a lemon to the taste of whipped cream. Compare the sound of meat frying and popcorn popping. Discuss what happens when water is heated. Compare the sound of an electric can opener with a blender or cake mixer. Have your child feel warm water and cold water. Have your child watch what happens when dishwater detergent is poured into a sink while water is running.

Flour Trays. Scoop some flour on a tray, paper plate, or baking sheet. Let your child play in the flour with their hands. Let them experiment with drawing and making designs. Add different measuring tools or little toys. For a different feeling and experience, add a little water to the flour until it has a *doughy* texture. They will have fun using their imagination to make different shapes with flour or dough.

Touching Texture Jars. Using empty baby food or canning jars, fill each jar with two to four ounces of items such as dry rice, lima beans, dry peas, kidney beans, and miniature marshmallows. Let them spend time feeling the items in the jars.

Slime Bag. Place three to four tablespoons of hair gel or whipped shaving cream in a sandwich-size plastic bag. It's less messy in a plastic bag, but what fun squishing the slime in the plastic bag with nothing to clean up after playtime.

Wet Paper Fun. What child does not like to play in water? Fill a small plastic tub, medium size container, or small bowl with water. Cut strips or tear pieces of paper from an old magazine and newspaper. Direct your child to put the paper in the water. Make sure they feel the paper when it is dry before the paper is placed in the water. Talk with them about how the paper feels after it is laced in the water.

Touching Experiences. There are opportunities for safe touches in your kitchen such as feeling whipped cream, rubbing grains of salt between fingers, and touching flour, a wet and dry dish cloth, rice, beans, and lettuce leaves. Also, your child will enjoy banging pots and lids together and squishing their hands in mashed potatoes or applesauce. Have your child touch wooden, plastic, and metal spoons. Have your child touch a slice of untoasted bread and toasted bread. Touch a stick of refrigerated butter and room-temperature butter.

Plant a Garden. This activity can be done together and involves ongoing senses. Digging in dirt, sorting seeds, watering, and smelling the flowers or herbs you plant will stimulate all senses.

Hearing Experiences. Your child will enjoy beating the bottom of a plastic bowl and a metal pot with a wooden spoon. Or, listening to water boiling in a pan, an alarm going off on the oven, the noise of a microwave oven running, the sound of water going down the drain, and a dishwasher going through its cleaning cycle. The opening and closing of drawers and cabinet doors. Kitchen floors being swept, kitchen clock ticking, or an oven timer beeping and toast popping up in a toaster.

Sound Tubes. Save a few empty paper towel rolls. Place a collection of uncooked rice, dried beans, and beads in a roll (one item in each roll). Seal the ends of the tubes with duct tape or packing tape. Let your child listen to the different sounds while shaking the rolls.

Homemade Musical Instruments. Children can create instruments from empty boxes and other items found around the house. Consider making maracas with dried beans, a paper cup, and wax paper, or a guitar from an empty tissue box and rubber bands. Also, an empty oatmeal box makes a perfect drum.

These are a small selection of sensory experiences in one room of your home. Just imagine the experiences other rooms in your home will provide for your child. The only limiting factor is doing something that might be unsafe. Otherwise, your home and backyard are treasures and excellent learning laboratories to stimulate children's senses.

Now that you have completed the self-assessment and discussed the environmental factors that promote learning in the home, you will need to determine whether your child and children are developmentally ready for acquiring prereading skills. There are prereading behaviors, or signs of readiness, for different ages and stages of growth. Let's examine signs and behaviors of prereading readiness to help you gauge where your child is developmentally.

IS MY CHILD READY?

Questions that parents and caregivers may face and ponder are, *When do we start introducing reading?* and *How do we know when our children are ready?* Some parents and caregivers choose to read to their children before they are born, and others begin reading to their children before they can focus on pages of a book or hold their heads up. According to Jana and Shu (2021), starting early with reading doesn't guarantee that your child will be significantly smarter or well read. However, introducing your child to reading will promote benefits such as strengthening bonding, nurturing a love for reading, and providing early exposure to language.

Parents and caregivers can encourage an early interest in reading by implementing these activities that nurture and help develop preliteracy skills in children. These recommended activities are simple and easy to incorporate during children's early learning years beginning with their birth. Make these activities a part of your daily schedule. By doing so, they will become a natural part of your family. They are:

- Have frequent conversations with your child.
- Sing songs.
- Ask your child to retell a story.
- Learn fingerplays.
- Create a book corner in your child's bedroom.
- Play language games such as rhymes and riddles.
- Model a love for books by reading books yourself.
- Make up your own stories.
- Point out road signs while driving.
- Tell your child the author and illustrator of the book and what they do.
- Ask your child to identify the author and illustrator of the book.
- Bake cookies in the shape of different letters.
- Clap to different rhythms and songs.
- Play an auditory story or read it out loud, and then discuss the story.
- Ask questions about the stories you read.
- Make up a story with a beginning, middle, and end.
- Point to parts of a word and what the sound is.
- Do the Hokey-Pokey dance.
- Play Simo Says by using body parts.
- Paint rocks with each letter of the alphabet.
- Play matching games with your child.
- Show your child a picture. Come up with a story about that picture.
- Put labels on common household items.
- Have your child write their name on each picture they draw.
- Have your child create a storybook with pictures and words.
- Let your child tell you a story from pictures in a book.
- Make letterboards for your child.
- Play games involving letters and sounds.
- Write a letter to a family member.
- Play with foam and plastic letters.
- Complete an alphabet puzzle.
- Make up a rhyming song together.
- Write letters in a tray of salt.
- Read instructions out loud to show their importance.
- Connect dots to make up letters and words.
- Say a sound and have your child guess the letter and vice versa.
- Tell a story without an ending and have your child make up the end.

Sowdon (2018), however, recommends parents and caregivers stop worrying and pushing three-, four-, and five-year-olds into reading programs before they are ready. According to Sowdon (2018), reading readiness can be divided into two categories—physical and language. She advises that no formal reading instruction should take place until reading readiness-related physical and language skills are exhibited. The process of learning to read can go more smoothly and quickly when children are allowed time to develop the physical and language skills needed to support reading. The physical and language signs parents and caregivers can look for to determine readiness are:

Physical Signs of Reading Readiness

- *Can your child skip using the opposite sides of the body? Can your child swing one arm while hopping on the other foot?* If your child can perform this skipping activity, it indicates there's a connection between the left and right sides of the body. If they are unable to skip, show them how to skip by starting with hopping on one foot and then the other foot to get them started. Note: If your child has a disability and skipping isn't feasible, use hand-clapping games where they clap and then slap hands with a partner in a rhythmic pattern.
- *Can your child cross the midline?* Does your child reach across his or her body with one hand, grasp an item, and bring it back across the body without switching hands? Younger children whose brains haven't developed will change hands when crossing their bodies. Being able to cross the body without switching hands demonstrates that the brain doesn't have trouble shifting an item from left to right or right to left. This skill correlates with eyes moving reading words from left to right across the page of a book.
- *Can your child follow an object with their eyes?* Hold a small toy or pencil about twelve inches from your child's face at nose level. Move the object across the line of sight from left to right and right to left. Watch the eyes to see if they smoothly follow the item without jumping. If their eyes "jump" when crossing the midline, they'll have trouble tracking words across the page.
- *Can your child stand on one foot for ten seconds with eyes both open and shut?* If your child struggles with balancing on one foot, he or she has not developed the brain and body connection needed for reading. The closed eyes test indicates having a good sense of where their body is in space without visual cues. If a child needs visual cues to stand still, stand on one foot, or perform other physical activities, they may not have the extra energy needed to focus on reading. They use their eyes to help maintain body awareness. Yoga is helpful with this problem.

- *Can your child draw themselves with at least ten body parts without cues or prompts?* See if your child knows his or her body parts and places the parts where they should be on a sheet of paper. This indicates if a child's brain is ready to see the differences in letters. If your child has difficulty, provide additional practice through games that require them to build a body. Also, point out the child's body parts as he or she plays the game. Then have the child draw himself or herself on paper.

Language Signs of Reading Readiness

- *Does your child look at books and words?* Does your child show an interest in reading? Does he or she *read* with you? Does he or she turn the pages or look at and point to the pictures on the page in their favorite book?
- *Can your child make rhymes and play word games?* Children who can hear the ending sounds of words can make up rhymes. Can he or she say a word that begins with the same sound as the word you say in a word game? Can he or she tell you whether the two words you say are the same or different? Hearing how words sound (same or different) and rhyming are important for understanding phonemes, sounds, and letter associations.
- *Can your child identify a variety of shapes? Can your child use prepositions?* Can your child name and identify different shapes he or she sees? Also, if you draw a circle and a square on a sheet of paper, can he or she tell you if the square is above, below, beside, or on top of the circle? The differences between letter shapes are subtle. Children need to see differences in shapes and sizes before being introduced to letters.
- *Can your child identify letters?* Your child needs to be able to identify a majority of the letters by name or sound before reading instruction begins. There are different views on which letter you should start teaching first. The important thing is knowing greater than half of the alphabet letters on sight.
- *Can your child read his or her name?* The first word children can read is their name. If you write your child's name along with a brief message, does he or she read the name and ask what the other words say? Children who respond in this manner realize the marks on the paper have meaning and are interested in the meaning of the other words.

Next, the focus is more on developing and laying the foundation for reading with children during the toddler stage (ages one to three), late preschool (age four), and kindergarten (age five). There is a brief discussion about the behaviors exhibited by children less than a year old (infancy) and what parents and caregivers can do to support early book behaviors exhibited.

Knowing and watching for early book behaviors will give parents and caregivers an idea of where their children are developmentally as well as what they can do to support the beginning stages of prereading skill development. Following is a brief description of behaviors exhibited by infants.

- *Around three months.* Babies begin to babble and smile at the sound of their parents' or caregivers' voices. At this time, babies should be able to hold their heads higher than in past months. Babies will better be able to grasp what you're saying and notice the expressions on your face. They may even attempt to touch the book or bring it to their mouths.
  - *What parents and caregivers can do.* Read aloud with your child snuggled in your lap. Select a board or soft book to read to your child and let them touch the book if they try to grasp the book. Read with expression and change your voice for each character in the stories and make appropriate sounds, if applicable.
- *Around six to twelve months.* Between these ages, your child will develop the ability to sit up tall with a steady head and grab the pages of the book being read. This is a behavior that indicates your child is interested in the book and may want to explore the book further by putting the book in his or her mouth. Additionally, they can copy looks on faces, copy sounds, and pay attention for a few minutes at a time.
  - *What parents and caregivers can do.* Continue reading to your child. Purchase books that are durable, colorful, with simple objects, and photographed faces at this age. Books will need to be able to withstand drooling and teeth marks during this time. Pay attention to the pictures your child is interested in. Act out pictures using your face, hands, and voice.
- *Around twelve months.* Your child should be able to sit up and hold the book with both hands. Also, he or she should be able to hold the book and turn the pages of the book as it is read. He or she may also carry his or her favorite book around and hand the book to you to read. Make note of their favorite books and expose them to a variety of other books.
- *Around twelve to eighteen months.* Your child should not only be sitting up without support but also be able to hold a board book with both hands. Additionally, he or she should be able to turn pages and point to pictures. They may also request that you read another book. Also, your child may point to a familiar animal and make the sound.
  - *What parents and caregivers can do.* Read to your children daily. Expose your children to books that have bright colorful pictures. As the reader, point to the pictures, talk about them, and describe what is hap-

pening on the page. Take your children to a local library for storytime. Also, talk to your child and surround them with language daily.

- *Around eighteen to twenty-three months.* Your child will be able to choose a book to be read but can point to a picture and say a few words about the picture. Also, your child can finish sentences from a book they know well.
  - ○ *What parents and caregivers can do.* Help your child pronounce words better by imitating their mispronounced words and then pronouncing the word correctly. Additionally, parents and caregivers can increase their child's understanding by speaking slowly, using short sentences, and waiting patiently for a response from their child. Book sharing can be used as a strategy to calm children and prepare them for a nap or bedtime.
- *Around two to three years old (toddlers).* Your child will be moving around more and will be more aware of their surroundings and self. He or she will be able to find objects for you and name body parts. Also, he or she will be able to play matching games, sort shapes, and play with simple puzzles.
  - ○ *What parents and caregivers can do.* Read to your children daily and set up a special time to read with them. Encourage your children to explore and try new words. Develop your children's language by talking and adding to words they say. Expand your children's knowledge of objects and items by pointing and naming them in books or pointing at them in the house. Teach your children to sing simple songs, learn simple nursery rhymes, and easy fingerplays.
- *Around three to four years old.* Your child will be more physical and independent. He or she will ask more questions about things around them. Continue to nurture a love for reading by taking them to the library.
  - ○ *What parents and caregivers can do.* You can continue to read to your children daily and provide experiences to promote an interest in reading by being a role model for your children. Let your children see you reading and select books to purchase. Write brief messages or notes so your children understand and know that the letters represent words and ideas. Continue developing language skills by speaking in complete sentences to your children. Also, use grown-up words and encourage your children to speak in complete sentences.

Here are additional typical signs that your three-, four-, or five-year-old will display when they are developing their literacy skills.

Three- and Four-Year-Olds

- Has one or two favorite books or rhymes
- Points out to you when you make an error reading their favorite story

- Enjoys new stories and asks a lot of questions
- Can sequence the events in a story
- Enjoys listening to bedtime stories
- Knows the letters of their name
- Can *write* by scribbling
- Can find a book when asked

Four- and Five-Year-Olds

- Knows their favorite book by name
- Knows a certain section of their favorite book
- Prefers one book over another
- Has a certain reading routine they follow at home and school
- Knows the purpose of reading
- Understands that the story remains the same
- Talks about the story sequence

Children experience and achieve many developmental milestones from birth to four years of age. This is a critical time for parents and caregivers to lay a solid foundation for learning to read. Knowing, understanding, and recognizing some of the behaviors related to reading will enable parents and caregivers to support and encourage prereading skill behaviors exhibited by their children. Also, parents and caregivers will be able to select and implement activities that align with their child's and children's prereading skill stage.

Another important environmental factor as a part of setting the stage for learning is the home. We have explored parents and caregivers and their children's readiness for learning as an aspect of setting the stage. Our next focus is on where the learning takes place in the home. Questions that may arise are: *Do we need a particular room in the home for learning to occur? Do we need specific equipment and learning tools to assist us? Do we need a special setup or room arrangement?* The answers to these questions will be addressed in the upcoming section of this chapter.

THE PHYSICAL HOME ENVIRONMENT: IS MY HOME READY?

The physical environment for infants, toddlers, and preschoolers is of the utmost importance during their early growth. Parents and caregivers need to do everything possible to ensure the safety of their children. Once young children become more mobile and independent it becomes necessary to implement safety measures such as plugs for electrical outlets and gates to block access to stairs. Heavy and sharp objects are placed out of the reach of curious little hands. Sharp-edged furniture is covered or moved to protect the unsteady gait of new walkers.

As children progress through infancy and preschool age, parents and caregivers need to have as many child-friendly rooms as possible. Providing low shelves, hooks, and child-size chairs and tables will accommodate their children's natural curiosity and growing independence. Engaging children in their home environment in a positive manner will stimulate their interest, curiosity, and exploratory nature. Place a variety of age-appropriate materials, children's books, supplies, and activities in several rooms, if possible. There is no specific number of rooms needed to create a positive learning environment in the home.

Purchasing electronic devices, games, and manipulatives such as puzzles, pegboards, and lacing bead tools will enhance parents' and caregivers' effectiveness and support. However, the most important element is a parent's and caregiver's direct involvement with his or her child. To effectively implement the plan to lay a foundation to raise a reader depends on the parents' and caregivers' commitment to setting aside the time needed to work with their children. Also needed is a commitment to implement the recommended prereading skills activities outlined in this resource handbook.

CHAPTER 2 SUMMARY

Chapter 2 centered on establishing the footing needed to support the framework for developing a strong reading foundation at home. The importance of parents' and caregivers' self-assessment was addressed through a series of questions to promote and generate reflective thoughts about learning in the home. Also, prereading readiness behaviors and milestones were shared to assist parents and caregivers to help them determine their children's readiness stage. A variety of suggested activities related to each developmental milestone were included to guide parents and caregivers with age-appropriate support and follow-up for their children.

Additionally, physical and language prereading readiness signs were discussed to provide parents and caregivers with additional behaviors to look for to assist them in supporting and extending their children's exposures and experiences in the home. Included in this chapter were selected examples of sensory activities parents and caregivers can implement to motivate and stimulate an interest in learning and reading. The author shared selected recommendations for making rooms in the home safe for children as they progressed from birth to preschool age.

The upcoming section, chapter 3, will present the first layer of the guided reading foundation plan: letter recognition and identification. Letter identification is the first prereading skill that is an essential component for learning how to read. The importance of letter identification and letter discrimination will be discussed and explored by the author.

Chapter Three

What They See

Visual Recognition and Discrimination of Letters

The earliest predictor of children's ability to learn how to read is their knowledge and understanding of the relationship between letters, letter sounds, and words. Children's difficulty with learning to read is often related to a lack of letter knowledge. Until children can name and identify letters of the alphabet and apply the alphabetic principle, letter knowledge, sound association, and word meanings, they will struggle with the reading process. A lack of letter knowledge and understanding of alphabet letters hinders the acquisition of reading.

According to Shanahan (2021), there are differing opinions among literacy experts and teachers on whether letter names or letter sounds should be taught first. Despite the differences of opinion, it was noted that many children learn and come to school knowing the letters when they begin preschool or kindergarten. Shanahan (2021) recommends beginning with letter names first and then adding letter name sounds next to eliminate confusion for young children who have short attention spans. However, he suggests that children's background knowledge of letters and sounds should be the determining factor to decide the starting point of instruction.

Also, recognizing the phonetic sounds of letters and associating them with words, lead the way to an essential tool for future readers—sounding out words. Consequently, the first step in children's reading journey for this plan is learning to recognize letters. No matter where your children are in their reading journey, all children begin with learning the alphabet. Learning the alphabet letters (uppercase and lowercase) is a great way to strengthen one of the fundamental skills of reading. It is extremely important to provide children with the appropriate exposure to enable them to acquire knowledge and an understanding of the alphabet letters.

Additionally, if children exhibit interest in letters in print, it is never too early to introduce them to learning the alphabet. This plan to raise readers at home begins with laying the first layer of the reading foundation—*a print-rich environment*. Parents and caregivers can successfully obtain and provide the first layer of the reading foundation. They can create a print-rich environment by exposing and surrounding children with a wealth of print experiences and activities at home. A print-rich environment includes books in the home, reading aloud to children, posting letters on the refrigerator, and engaging in reading activities themselves.

Other activities that enrich children's environment with print are pointing out the letters in their first name, on street signs, restaurants, grocery stores, addresses, shopping malls, road signs, billboards, traffic signs, cereal boxes, canned goods, visits to the library, attending storytimes, reading cards received, posting notes, and on canned goods. Parents and caregivers have an unlimited supply of print available to them as resources. It will be up to each parent and caregiver to utilize their home and outside environment as their print-rich environmental backdrop and learning laboratory. Commitment to emphasizing the importance of print daily is necessary.

Since all children's path to reading begins with their letter knowledge, parents and caregivers may have questions about teaching the alphabet letters. Should uppercase or lowercase alphabet letters be taught first? Should alphabet letters be taught as they appear in their alphabetical order? Are there any alphabet letters that are difficult for children to learn? What are experts in the field saying about teaching letter names to children? A review of the literature indicates a debate over which form of the alphabet letter to teach first. Although lowercase letters are present more visually, uppercase letters are easier to tell apart from one another.

It is also recommended not to teach the letters as they appear in the alphabet. The letters that appear the beginning of the alphabet are easy to learn. However, although they are easy to learn, the beginning letters of the alphabet (a, b, c, d, e) are not the most beginning letter of sight words children will learn. Parents and caregivers should focus first on teaching the alphabet letters most common in the beginning of sight words. Most used letters to teach are m, s, f, c, p, and t. Teach least commonly used letters last such as q, v, z, and x.

Sarah (2023), a former kindergarten teacher and author of *How Wee Learn,* recommends parents and caregivers first wait until little minds have ample time to hear different words and sounds. The first group of letters Sarah advises parents and caregivers to teach are SATIN. By learning these letters letters first, children are able to blend and combine the letters that make up the word families at, an, it, ip, ap, and in. Outlined next is a detailed explanation of the order the letters can be taught. *Note:* The letter and vowel sounds are taught along with the letter names starting with the short vowels first in this method. Phonemic awareness (letter sounds) and auditory discrimination (short and long vowels) will be covered in chapter 4.

s-a-t-p-i-n

First, start with s, a, t, p, i, n. This combination of letters is perfect for introducing letter names and sounds and then actually *applying* what you are teaching. This way, when your child starts to apply their knowledge of letters and sounds, they will be able to start reading simple words more quickly.

c-o-d-g-m-k

The next letters are necessarily more available in sight words. Knowledge of these additional letters will enable children to start spelling simple cvc (consonant-vowel-consonant) words. Additionally, children are exposed to a wider variety of words that can help them start to read.

e-r-u-b-h-f-l

These letters add the rest of the vowels and add on to the letters previously learned.

j-w-v-x-y-z-q

These letters show up least frequently in words. This does not, however, make them less important than the other letters. Practice these letters as much as possible along with the other letters learned.

Parents and caregivers need to decide which letter name instruction and sequence to use before beginning letter name instruction. Key to any decision made is your child's developmental stage, interest, and motivation. Select what is best for your child based on his or her individual needs. Be tuned into all aspects of your child's growth and development. Parents and caregivers know their children better than anyone else. Exercise your right to decide which procedures, methods, or instructional activities best meet your children's educational needs.

Additionally, parents and caregivers need to understand what letter name knowledge is. Letter-name knowledge consists of two parts—recognizing letters and naming letters. For example, show your child the letters *M*, *S*, and *T* and ask him or her to point to the letter is *S*, he or she recognizes letter *S* if he or she points to the *S*. An example of naming a letter occurs when you point to or hold up a letter and your child says the name (orally) of the letter held up or pointed to. Parents and caregivers will be involved in both aspects of letter knowledge in this section of the raising readers at home plan.

The first step of alphabet letter knowledge is to determine your child's current letter knowledge level. If you are not sure of where your child is with his or her knowledge of the alphabet letters, next is a checklist to help you assess where your child is and what activities you can implement to assist your children in mastering and maintaining their alphabet knowledge. Just knowing how to sing the *Alphabet Song* is not an indicator of letter knowledge by itself. Following are five signs that you can use to gauge your children's letter knowledge. Alphabet letter knowledge activities follow the letter knowledge checklist.

CHECKLIST FOR YOUR CHILDREN'S LETTER KNOWLEDGE

- Your child can recite the alphabet song. Yes/No
- Your child recognizes the *capital letters*. For example, if asked to point to *M*, he or she can. Yes/No
- Your child recognizes *lowercase letters*. If asked to point to *s*, he or she can. Yes/No
- Your child *notices letters* in his or her environment, such as book covers, store signs, and street signs. Yes/No
- Your child knows the most common sounds of the letters. For example, the letter B says /b/ as in *ball* and *bell*. Yes/No

Remember children develop and learn at different ages, stages, and rates. Do not compare one child's progress and accomplishments with another child. This statement applies to siblings in the same family as well as relatives and neighborhood friends. Let each child's progress and growth be the main guiding force to work with your children. Utilizing the letter name checklist will assist you in determining if you need to spend more time exposing your children to environmental print before implementing the letter games. This plan is designed to meet the individual developmental and intellectual needs of children.

This chapter is divided into two sections to accommodate children's different letter knowledge and letter readiness levels. It is strongly recommended that you do the exercises designed for children who are at the beginning stages and are just exhibiting some interest in the alphabet letters. The second section is designed for children who know over half of the alphabet letters and have demonstrated a high-level interest in letters and words. This section will also incorporate words that begin or end with selected alphabet letters. Both sections, however, will expose children to forming, saying, and writing the alphabet letters.

For parents and caregivers whose children need additional environmental print and letter name experiences, the author strongly suggests using the additional letter name hands-on exercises *before* beginning to formal letter name instruction. Alphabet knowledge is a necessary component in the formation of the reading foundation. Taking the extra time needed to acquire the recognition and knowledge of most of the alphabet letters will foster success and increase motivation. Here are several easy-to-do hands-on activities to build and strengthen letter knowledge. Directions and suggested materials needed are provided for each activity.

These activities are presented and strongly recommended for children that know fewer than eleven alphabet letters (uppercase or lowercase). However, children that know and recognize twelve or more alphabet letters may perform these activities to maintain and provide additional practice, if needed.

SECTION 1: GAMES AND ACTIVITIES TO INCREASE ALPHABET LETTER KNOWLEDGE

Sing-Along *Alphabet Song*

Instructions: Cut two strings of yarn, ropes, twine, or clothesline for the sing-along letter game. On one string attach the capital (uppercase) letters and on the other string attach the lowercase (small letters). Place the alphabet letters on cardstock, index cards, or construction paper. Also, alphabet cards may be printed electronically or purchased commercially in any local store. Attach the cards alphabetically in order using a stapler or tape. Punch a hole in the center top of each index card or cardstock with a hole puncher and then tie each card to the string.

Materials Needed: Yarn, twine, rope, ribbon, or clothesline. *Note:* The length of string needed is determined by how close the cards are placed on the string being used.

Implementation: Once the uppercase and lowercase strings are completed, you may sing the alphabet song and point to each letter as you say the letter name in the song. Encourage your child to sing along with you as you point to the letters. Work with the uppercase and lowercase separately until your child recognizes most of the letters on his or her own.

Environment Print Notebook

Instructions: Collect and create a notebook of environmental print.

Materials Needed: Old magazines, newspapers, ads, books, downloaded images, scissors, notebook (optional size), and tape or glue.

Implementation: Place a variety of pictures of environmental print in a notebook to expose your child to print in their immediate environment. Draw their attention to printed words seen in their home as well as in other places outside of the home—stores, restaurants, traffic signs, street signs, billboards, and work signs. Point out the letters as he or she "reads" the environment print.

Alphabet Books

Instructions: Alphabet books can be purchased in low-cost stores such as Dollar Tree and Dollar General. You can make your alphabet book by collecting cut letters, words, and pictures of items that begin with each alphabet letter (uppercase and lowercase). See the example pictured here.

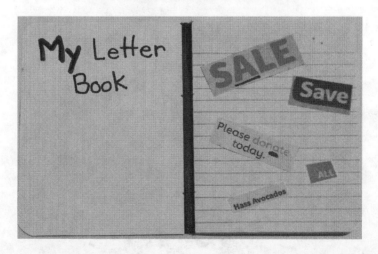

Feeling Alphabet Letters

Instructions: Purchase a pack of index cards or cardstock paper (any color) to create *feely* uppercase and lowercase alphabet cards for your child. Using paste or glue, write/form each letter with your finger or a brush. Sprinkle glitter on the glue or paste and let dry. Shake off the excess glitter. Other materials that can cover the letter are peas, rice, and baby lima beans. Store the letters in a plastic container.

Materials Needed: Index cards or cardstock paper, glue or paste, glitter, small lima beans, peas, or rice, and a plastic container or bag for the feely alphabet letters.

Implementation: Say the name of the letter and trace or touch the letter with your finger. Repeat this step and use your child's finger to trace or touch the letter as you say the name of the letter. Make sure your child says the name of the letter with you. Repeat this procedure as many times as needed until your child can point to and say the names of the letters you say. Feeling the letters (sensory) help children remember the names of the letters and their formation. These letters can also be used to match uppercase letters with their lowercase counterpart.

Alphabet Letter Hunt

Instructions: Make or purchase ready-made alphabet letters (uppercase and lowercase) for this activity. Using a magnetic clip or clothespin, select two letters for your child to hunt daily. Your child can look for the letters in the house or in the environment (street and road signs, grocery store, cereal boxes, magazines, newspapers, and books). Increase the number of letters your child is directed to hunt depending on their progress with learning the letters. Also, always include alphabet letters mastered with new alphabet letters being learned for continuous review and reinforcement. Be sure to keep up with the alphabet letters that are hard to learn.

Materials Needed: Alphabet letter cards, magnetic clips or magnetic letters, magnetic board or cookie sheet, clothespins, and hangers (optional). See the pictured examples provided (hanger clothespins, and magnetic board).

I Spy Letter Activity

Instructions: Select letters for recognition and identification.

Materials Needed: A toy pair of binoculars (optional), a magnifying glass, or an empty paper towel roll (spyglass).

Implementation: Looking through the spyglass, say, "I spy a letter. The letter is at the beginning of the word 'tub.'" Tell me the name of the letter and see if you can find it. *Note:* This game can be played inside the home, outside during walks, and in stores or malls. As your child progresses, encourage him or her to lead the game.

Alphabet Letter Bowling Game

Instructions: Children *strike* or hit the letter called with a small ball.

Materials Needed: Medium-sized paper cups (for uppercase and lowercase letters), a small ball, and a blacker marker.

Implementation: Line up the cups in random order three to four inches apart. Say the name of a letter and direct your child to hit the cup that has the letter named. Variations for this game are lining up the lowercase letters and saying the name of a letter and telling your child to strike the lowercase form of the letter. Also, say a word and have your child strike the letter that begins the word.

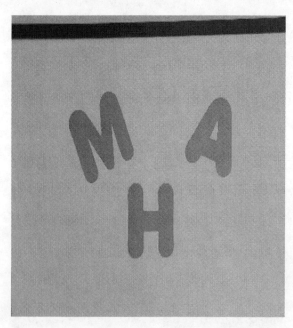

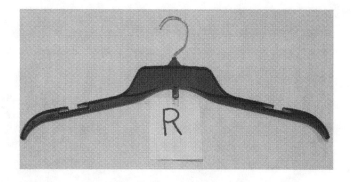

Lowercase Alphabet Match with a Game Board

Instructions: Match the uppercase letters with their corresponding lowercase letters.

Materials Needed: Universal game board, a set of uppercase and lowercase alphabet letters, marker, construction paper, and index cards (optional).

Implementation: Using the game board, write or put on cards the uppercase alphabet letters.

Direct your child to find the lowercase partner for each uppercase letter you place on the board. The lowercase form of the uppercase letter should be placed on top of the uppercase letter. *Note:* Use the same game board and replace the uppercase letters with lowercase letters. Begin again.

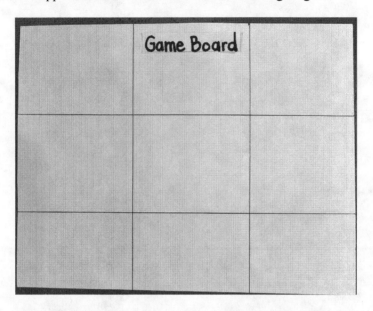

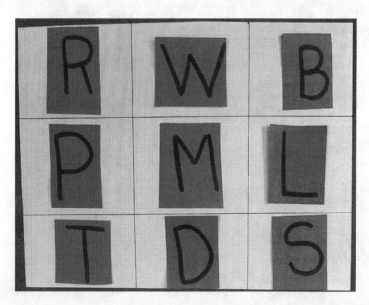

Note: For example, children find the lowercase alphabet letter for uppercase letters on the board.

Lowercase Alphabet Picture or Word Match Activity

Instructions: Find pictures or words that begin with selected lowercase alphabet letters.

Materials Needed: Game board (made or a plain sheet of paper), old magazines, ads, and scissors.

Implementation: Place selected alphabet letters on the game board. Direct your child to cut out two words or pictures that begin with the lowercase letters selected. See the example picture.

Note: Your child may draw pictures or search for items in the house beginning with the letter selected.

Shaving Cream or Whipped Cream Alphabet Letters

Instructions: Spray shaving cream or whipped cream on a flat covered surface or cookie sheet. Sing the *Alphabet Song* and form the letters in the shaving cream or whipped cream. Say the name of the letter as you form it in the creamy mixture.

Materials Needed: Shaving cream or whipped cream, rubber gloves (optional), cookie sheet, table, countertop, and an old adult t-shirt or an apron.

Implementation: Guide your child in forming the letters. (*Note:* Singing the *Alphabet Song* during this activity is optional.) You can simply say the name of the letters as you introduce each letter to your child. Also, remember to direct him or her to say the name of the letter after you. Your child will have fun learning the names of the alphabet letters (uppercase and lowercase). To avoid messing up clothing, have them wear a full-body apron or an old adult t-shirt. Another option for you is to wear a pair of rubber gloves and an apron. Additionally, place newspaper or any other covering to protect your floor. This activity is perfect for outside during clear and sunny weather.

Playdough Alphabet Letters

Instructions: Purchase playdough and make the alphabet letters for your children. They will have fun naming and making the letters with your assistance until they can form the letters on their own.

Materials Needed: Commercial playdough. *Note:* You may purchase a variety of colors.

Implementation: Say the name of each letter as you form the letter. Direct your child to say the name of the letter after you. See if he or she can find the letter in a magazine, newspaper, or book. Make sure your child has mastered a letter before you go on to the next letter. You may work with more than one letter during a session depending on how your child progresses. Provide practice throughout the day.

Homemade Playdough (Optional)

Instructions: Add more experiences with the playdough alphabet letter activity by making homemade playdough and including your child in the process.

Materials Needed: Two cups of all-purpose (plain) flour, two tablespoons of oil (vegetable, coconut, or olive), one cup of salt, two tablespoons of cream of tartar, two cups of water, and food coloring (color of your choice). In a medium size pot, add the flour, salt, cream of tartar, oil, and water. Mix and stir the playdough. Next, place the pot on the stove on low/medium heat. Stir the mixture continuously until the mixture thickens and becomes *doughy*. Remove the dough from the heat.

Place the dough on a covered board, counter, or table. Allow the dough to cool for a few minutes and knead the playdough like bread. *Note:* You may divide the dough into sections. Add drops of food coloring (optional) and knead the dough until the dough is colored. Store the playdough in plastic bags or containers. Coloring the playdough will make the activity even more fun and provide an opportunity to teach color recognition too.

Implementation: Follow the same procedure outlined for commercial playdough. Consider making all uppercase alphabet letters one color and all lowercase letters a different color.

To add variety and extend the activity, direct your child to name the letter formed and point to or find something in your home that is the same color as the playdough. An additional alternate activity for this playdough alphabet letter is blindfolding your child before you form a letter. After forming the letter, hold your child's hand and trace the letter with his or her hand. See if your child can say the name of the letter. *Note:* Do this activity after they have mastered several alphabet letters to have a better level of success.

Alphabet Necklace or Bracelet

Instructions: You and your child can keep up with the letters learned or are learning with an alphabet bracelet or necklace. This is another excellent way to help your child maintain the knowledge of the letters he or she has learned.

Materials Needed: Craft string, yarn, twine, or ribbon, one pack of 4-×-6-inch index cards or craft tags, one single-hole punch, a pair of scissors, and a black magic marker or crayon.

Implementation: Cut each index card into four quarters (2 × 3 inches) and place a single hole in the top center of each card. Write an alphabet letter on each card or craft tag. As your child learns the name of and recognizes each letter, add the letter to the necklace/bracelet. Determine how long you want your child's necklace or bracelet to be. Cut the string to your desired length. As an alternative, write the uppercase letter on the front side of the card and write the lowercase letter on the back of the card. *Note:* Remember to add the cards as the letters are learned. These cards may also be used to practice saying and placing the letters in alphabetical order on or off the string.

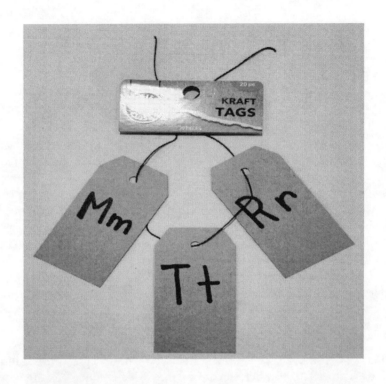

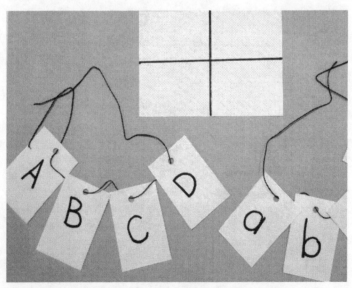

Cereal Box Alphabet Letter Hunt

Instructions: Save your empty cereal boxes. Use the outsides of the boxes to find and hunt selected alphabet letters of choice.

Materials Needed: Empty cereal box and a black magic marker or crayon.

Implementation: Direct your child to circle, underline, put an X, or point to the letter you say. This activity can be extended by underlining letters that need to be found in the house, during a neighborhood walk, or grocery shopping. See the pictured example.

Alphabet Letter Sheet Activity

Instructions: Save that old bedsheet and repurpose it to provide a fun activity to learn and improve alphabet letter knowledge.

Implementation: Write the uppercase and lowercase letters on the bedsheet. Spread the letters throughout the sheet randomly. Direct your child to walk or crawl to the letter name you call out to him or her. You can also say the name of an uppercase letter and have them find the lowercase letter. Extend the learning by asking them to say a word or find a picture that has the letter you named at the beginning or end. *Note:* This activity can be conducted inside the home or outside (weather permitting).

Alphabet Keyboard: Uppercase Letters Practice

Instructions: Old computer keyboards are perfect tools for learning and mastering letter names. If you don't have an old keyboard handy, visit your local thrift store and purchase a used cost-effective keyboard. Sanitize it thoroughly before allowing your child to use it.

Materials Needed: Keyboard (old or used) and alphabet letters (uppercase and lowercase).

Implementation: For new learners, say the name of a letter and have your child point to the letter named. After your child has learned the uppercase letters, point to an uppercase alphabet letter on the keyboard. Tell your child to find the lowercase form of the letter you point to or say.

Invisible Alphabet Letters Game

Instructions: Form the alphabet letters in the air.

Materials Needed: None or hold a pencil in your hand (optional).

Implementation: Stand or sit with your back facing your child. Hold your arm up a little above eye level and form the letter in the air. Ask your child to identify and say the name of the letter you formed in the air. You can extend this activity by directing your child to find the letter you wrote in the air in a magazine, newspaper, book, or any other appropriate material in your home. An alternative strategy is to *write* the letter on your child's back with your finger.

Name the Alphabet Letter

Instructions: Obtain a small brown bag and place uppercase or lowercase alphabet letters (cards/letter tiles) in the bag. *Note:* You make separate the uppercase and lowercase letters (a bag for each) or place the uppercase and lowercase letters in one bag.

Materials Needed: A small brown paper bag and a purchased set of uppercase and lowercase alphabet letters or letter tiles. *Note:* The alphabet letter cards can be purchased or made using cardstock or index cards.

Implementation: Put the cards in the bag and shake the bag vigorously to mix the letters. Ask your child to select a card and say the name of the letter he or she selected.

I Spy Neighborhood Walk

Instructions: Walk around your neighborhood or a nearby mall with your child.

Materials Needed: None.

Implementation: Walk with your child and say, "I spy the letter *L*. Find or point to the letter *L*."

Extension of the I Spy game: Find the uppercase letter *L only*. Find the lowercase *l*.

Feed the Alphabet Letter Fishbowl

Instructions: Keep track of the uppercase and lowercase alphabet letters learned and mastered.

Materials Needed: A small or medium size bowl or container of personal choice, cardstock or construction paper, black marker or a dark-colored crayon, and scissors.

Implementation: Trace a fish or other object of choice out of cardstock or construction paper. Write the uppercase and lowercase of each alphabet letter (total of fifty-two letters). As letters are mastered, direct your child to put the mastered *fish* alphabet letter in the bowl. To create a fish pattern, see the example shown. Make fifty-two fish. *Note:* You may use other items instead of fish.

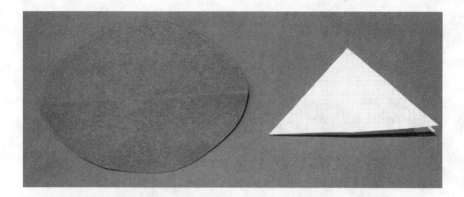

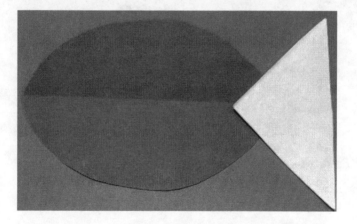

Trace the outline of the fish shape with a pencil, marker, or crayon. Cut out a small triangle to form a mouth for your fish (optional). Also, you determine the size of the fish you create for your child.

Alphabet Letter Match

Instructions: Match uppercase alphabet letters with their lowercase letter form.

Materials Needed: Cardstock paper (8.5 × 11 inches), single-hole punch, yarn or string, black marker or crayon, and tape.

Implementation: Fold the cardstock paper in half (lengthwise). On one side of the paper write the uppercase alphabet letter and on the other side of the paper, write the lowercase alphabet letter.

Punch a hole next to each alphabet letter. On the back side of the card, tape the yarn or string and pull it through the hole. *Note:* The yarn or string should reach from the left side to the right side.

For example, see views 1 and 2 of the Alphabet Letter Match Activity.

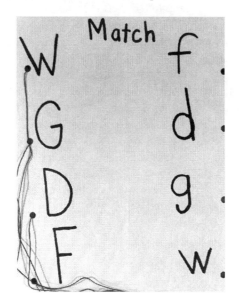

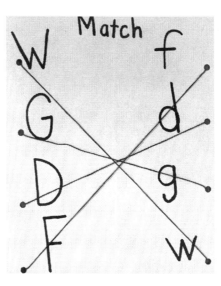

SECTION 2: ALPHABET LETTER
KNOWLEDGE ENHANCEMENT

The activities provided in this section are designed to extend and enhance children's experience with the letters and their sounds. Parents and caregivers are welcome to use the selected activities in Section 1 for review and maintenance of alphabet letters already known. The focus of Section 2 is on the sounds of the letters and words associated with those sounds. Additionally, children will continue learning letter names with increased exposure to different letter fonts found in assorted printed material.

If you are beginning in Section 2 Alphabet Letter Enhancement, your child already knows the names of over half of the alphabet letters. Congratulations on reaching this milestone. Your child has demonstrated a high level of interest in letters around his or her home and outside environment. We will continue your children's growth by including pictures that begin with the alphabet letters and words that have the alphabet letters in the beginning, middle, and end. Children will have more experiences and exposure to words in this part of the raising readers at home foundational plan.

Alphabet Paper Plate Games

Instructions: Collect images of items that begin with the alphabet letters.

Materials Needed: Scissors, clothes pins (clips), paper plates (size is optional), downloaded images or pictures from old magazines, ads, books, tape or glue, and newspapers.

Implementation: Write the uppercase and lowercase alphabet letters in the center of the paper plate. Glue or tape pictures to the clip end of the clothespin. Direct your child to select the picture of items that start with the letter in the center of the paper plate. Extension: Ask your child to find or draw pictures of items in the house that begin with the letter on the paper plate.

This activity can be extended by instructing your child to find words that begin or end with each selected letter.

Letter Search with a Variety of Print Fonts

Instructions: Gather words showing a selected letter in a variety of print fonts.

Materials Needed: Old magazines, newspapers, ads, construction paper or notebook, scissors, and glue.

Implementation: Find and cut out a variety of words with different print fonts for each alphabet letter. Place the collection of alphabet letter print fonts in a notebook or folder for review and practice. See example of Alphabet *Aa* Print Fonts Search.

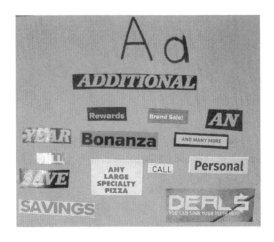

Egg Carton Alphabet Search

Instructions: Write a letter (uppercase or lowercase alphabet letter) on an empty egg carton. Children fill the egg carton with a word or item with the selected alphabet letter.

Materials Needed: Empty egg cartons, old magazines, newspapers, and scissors.

Implementation: Using a magic marker or crayon, write the alphabet letter on top of the carton. Direct your child to cut out pictures to fill the egg carton words that have the letter the word. *Extension:* Say the word found by your child and tell him or her to say the word after you. Use the word in a sentence to check his or her understanding of the word.

The activities presented in this chapter were designed to formulate the first layer of the foundation needed to raise a reader. If your child has not learned the alphabet letters (all fifty-two), repeat selected games and instructional games. Always keep in mind that children grow and learn at different rates and stages of their physical and intellectual development. Issues or concerns that are exhibited and exist for an extended period may warrant professional consultation and assistance.

CHAPTER 3 SUMMARY

The first important step to provide and build a solid foundation to raise a reader at home is letter recognition. Knowing and recognizing the letters of the alphabet is a key component of the reading process. Parents and caregivers play a vital role in nurturing and developing their children's interest in the world of print. By surrounding and exposing their children to print at home and in their outside environment, parents and caregivers model that letters forming words have meaning.

Chapter 3 presents recommendations and tips on how parents and caregivers can create and print-rich environment for children. Also, questions parents and caregivers may have about teaching the alphabet letters are explored and examined. Additionally, parents and caregivers are given a checklist consisting of questions to help them determine where their children are with alphabet letter recognition. Assessing children's letter recognition knowledge helps parents and caregivers determine the starting point for the first layer needed to raise a reader at home—a strong foundation. Letter recognition and letter discrimination are necessary for developing readers.

Parents and caregivers are exposed to different methods of sequencing the letters when presenting and teaching the alphabet letters to their children. Also, children's physical signs of readiness for acquiring letter knowledge are shared to give parents and caregivers additional pointers to gauge their child's readiness for alphabet letter formal instruction. It is noted, however, that parents and caregivers need to decide what is best for their children based on where they are developmentally. Children learn at different stages and rates. The instructional activities in this guide are designed to meet the various needs of parents and caregivers and their children.

Chapter Four

What They Hear

Phonemic Awareness and Auditory Discrimination

Letter-sound correspondence is a vital component of the process of learning to read. Children need to have the ability to hear, identify, and manipulate sounds in spoken words. Phonemic awareness is auditory and does not involve print. The phonemes (sounds) for letters are essential for reading and the teaching of phonics. Although our English alphabet only consists of twenty-six alphabet letters, there are forty-four phonemes (individual distinct units of sounds) children must master. Understanding and knowing the letter-sound correspondence will assist your children in becoming successful readers.

What is phonemic awareness and how does it relate to reading? Why is phonological and phonemic awareness necessary and the same? There is a difference between these two terms—phonological awareness and phoneme awareness. Both are about sounds and are necessary and integral parts of reading. Phonological awareness deals with large units of sound such as words and syllables. Phonemic awareness focuses on the smallest units of sounds associated with individual letters that make up words. Phonological awareness is the house and phonemic awareness is one of the rooms in the house. Both skills will make learning to read easier.

Parents and caregivers are laying down a foundation for reading by starting their children with the small and large units of sounds comprising words spoken during their developmental and early learning years. This section of the plan includes activities and instructional games that are designed to nurture and develop phonemic awareness and phonological awareness. The initial layer of the reading foundation focuses on alphabet letter recognition and letter discrimination. of alphabet letters.

According to Brooks (2020), letter-sound associations or correspondence should be taught along with the alphabet letter names. She states teaching

letter-sound correspondence along with letter identification augments phonemic awareness, phonics understanding, decoding words, and reading skills
overall. Also, Brooks (2020) recommends teaching the letter names and
their corresponding sounds one letter at a time. By doing so, children will
understand phonemic awareness and phonics which will help them become
successful readers.

Letter-sound correspondence is essential for reading and writing. For your
child to read, he or she must recognize the letters in the word and associate each letter with its sound. To write or type a word, children must break
the word into its component sounds and know the letters that represent the
sounds. These skills are the basic building blocks for literacy learning. These
skills along with phonological awareness are strong predictors of how well
children read. You are preparing your children well for their learning-to-read
journey.

An excellent starting point, for this section, is surveying your home to
see what you have that can be associated with sounds of the alphabet letters.
Next, start collecting pictures of objects or items representing a variety of letters and their sounds. Many pictures or images can be downloaded from the
internet or found in old newspaper ads, magazines, workbooks, and children's
coloring books. You can also search your child's favorite toys and books for
items to use during your instructional time. A collection of items the children
are familiar with will help cement their letter knowledge and its corresponding sounds on a personal and enjoyable level.

Once you have gathered specific items and resource materials to assist your
child's letter name and letter sound journey, you may begin. Here are some
suggestions for you to review and consider while working with letter-sound
correspondences with your children.

- Check to see if your child is aware and hears the differences in sounds of
  letters and words (phonological awareness). Example: Repeat two words
  can and *tan* or *boy* and *bell*. Ask your child if the words sound the same in
  the beginning or the end. Continue checking to see if your child hears that
  rhyme and words that begin or end with the same letter sounds. The following is a list of words to help you get started with checking your child's
  phonological awareness.

Phonological Awareness Checklist of Words

Say Sun
Tall Ball
Boat Moat

Car Cat
Not Cot
Tag Wag
Mat Milk
Fan Ban
Heat Meat
Red Run

- Use the letters in your child's first name to generate interest and motivate listening for sounds.
- Build in movement with the phonological practice activities to incorporate motor skills and body movement. For example, raise your hand if the words sound the same in the beginning. Stand up if the words sound the same in the beginning and sit down if they sound the same at the end. Make a circle in the air with your finger if the words sound the same at the beginning.
- Work with the letter sounds that are harder to hear last (*m, p, b, v*, etc.).
- Keep a record of the letter sounds your child has learned.
- Incorporate breaks between sessions working on letter sounds.
- Letters that look similar and have similar sounds (*b* and *d*) should be taught separately to avoid confusion.
- Short vowel sounds are taught before long vowel sounds.
- Teach the letters and their sounds that occur frequently in small words such as *a, m*, and *t*.

Name and Sound Alphabet Letter Search Game

Instructions: Make a *name* card with your child's first name. Teach one letter in the name at a time.

Materials Needed: One sheet of construction paper or cardstock (8.5 × 11 inches), a black marker or crayon, and a pair of scissors.

Implementation: Write your child's first name on one half of the sheet of cardstock or construction paper. After writing your child's first name on the paper, cut between each letter creating a puzzle. Teach the name and recognition of each letter (in order) until your child recognizes and can name the letters in his or her name. Have your child find each letter of his or her name in magazines, books, and newspapers. See the example of the name card.

Alphabet Name Card

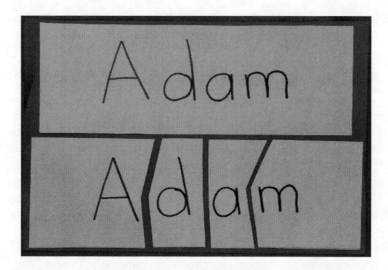

An Extension Activity for the Name Letter Search Game

Instructions: Select the consonant alphabet letters in your child's first name. Using the alphabet name card, the two consonant letters in *Adam* are *d* and *m*. Tell your child to find an item in the house or a picture in a book or magazine that begins or ends with the same sound. This name card activity also can be used when the vowels are discussed in chapter 5. However, if you have already been working with your child on long and short vowel sounds, you can include the vowel letters also.

Auditory Discrimination Listening Activities—Scripted Lesson

Instructions: Say the words aloud and pause (two to three seconds) after saying the first word. Repeat the words as often as needed.

Directions: Say: *I am going to say two words. Listen and tell me if the words are the same or different. If the words I say sound the same (alike), say Yes. If words I say are not the same (different), say No. Note:* Practice a few times to make sure your child understands the directions.
     Say: *Are you ready? Let's begin!*

1. bat . . . bat
2. cup . . . cat
3. four . . . feet

4. tip . . . tip
5. tub . . . top
6. sew . . . sew
7. far . . . far
8. hear . . . house

Auditory Discrimination Listening (Beginning Sounds) Activity— Scripted Lesson

Instructions: Read the pair of selected words. Say the words aloud and pause (two to three seconds) after saying the first word. Repeat the words as often as needed.

Directions: Say: *I am going to say two words. Listen for the sound you hear at the beginning of the two words I say. If you hear the same sound in the beginning of the two words I say, say Yes. If the two words I say do not have the same sound in the beginning, say No. Note:* You may add movement by having your child stand up, raise his or her hand, or clap when they hear the same sound in the beginning.

1. car . . . cat
2. rain . . . west
3. boat . . . box
4. top . . . toy
5. man . . . nail
6. wall . . . pat
7. jam . . . juice
8. horse . . . net
9. foot . . . fish
10. see . . . lip

Note: You may extend the level of difficulty of this listening activity by asking your child to draw or point to a picture that has the same sound in the beginning as the two words you stated.

Listening Beginning Sounds of Pictures Activity— Nonscripted Lesson

Instructions: Select a picture and repeat the name of the picture twice.

Materials Needed: Pictures of items from old magazines or downloaded images from the internet, index cards or cardstock, and glue or paste.

Directions: Collect two sets of matching pictures of familiar items for your child. Glue or paste each picture on an index card or cardstock. Set aside one set for you and place the other set before your child. Select a picture with the back of the picture card facing your child. Say the name of the item and ask your child to find the picture that begins with the sound they hear.

The Letter Sound of the Day

Instructions: Place the letter and letter sound of the day on your refrigerator or memo board.

Directions: Select a letter representing the letter sound you are teaching or reviewing in a selected spot in your home. During that entire day or week, direct your child to listen to the sound of the day or week. Make sure you keep a record of the letter sounds taught. Extend the level of difficulty by having your child say a word and draw or find a picture of items that represent the sound being learned that day or week. Next is an alternate way to highlight the letter sound.

Materials Needed: Styrofoam, plastic, or paper cup, popsicle sticks, and alphabet letters.

Note: The instructions and directions are the same as the Letter Sound of the Day. This alternate activity using a cup enables the parent/caregiver and child a visible picture of the sounds learned. Each letter and letter sound learned can be placed in another cup after demonstrating proficiency.

Rhyme Time (Ending Sounds)—Scripted Lesson

Instructions: Read the pair of selected words. Say the words aloud and pause (two to three seconds) after saying the first word. Repeat the words as often as needed.

Directions: Say: *Words can sound the same (alike) at the end. We say they rhyme when the words sound the same (alike) at the end.* Say: *Listen to these words I say. Cat . . . Hat. Say them with me. Cat . . . Hat. Cat and hat sound the same (alike) at the end. I am going to say more words. I want you to listen for how they sound at the end. Hold up one finger if the two words I say sound the same (alike) at the end. Note*: You may say the words rhyme.

Word List

1. book look
2. well let
3. mop top
4. fan can
5. sun run
6. cake lake
7. toe goat
8. see bee
9. tie pie
10. wall ball

Rhyming Riddles Time (Ending Sounds)—Scripted Lesson

Instructions: Repeat the riddle provided for your child. The answer is specified.

Directions: Say: *I am going to play a rhyming guessing game (riddle) with you. I will give help (you guess the answer). The answer will sound the same at the end and rhyme with the word I say to help you.* Say: *I am thinking of a word that sounds the same as cat at the end (rhymes) and it is something you wear on your head. What am I thinking of? (Answer: hat).* Say: *Hat and cat have the same sound at the end. Let's try other rhyming riddles. Note.* You may create your own riddles to provide additional practice. Also, introduce words that sound alike at the end as rhymes.

Rhyming Riddles

1. I am thinking of a word that sounds like door at the end (rhymes with) and you walk on it. What word am I thinking of? (Answer: floor).
2. I am thinking of a word that sounds like red at the end (rhymes with) and you lay on it to sleep. What word am I thinking of? (Answer: bed).
3. I am thinking of something you put on your feet before your put on your shoes and sounds like clocks at the end (rhymes with). What word am I thinking of? (Answer: socks)
4. I am thinking of a word that sounds like willow at the end (rhymes with) and it is something you put your head on in bed. What word am I thinking of? (Answer: pillow).
5. I am thinking of a word that sounds like tight at the end (rhymes with) what you turn on in a dark room. (Answer: light)
6. I am thinking of a word that sounds like sing at the end (rhymes with) and it is something you wear on your finger. What word am I thinking of? (Answer: ring)
7. I am thinking of a word that sounds like all at the end (rhymes with) and is something you throw or bounce. What word am I thinking of? (Answer: ball)
8. I am thinking of a word that sounds like coat at the end (rhymes with) that you ride in on water. (Answer: boat)
9. I am thinking of a word that sounds like lot at the end (rhymes with) and is something food is cooked in. (Answer: pot)
10. I am thinking of a word that sounds like bee at the end (rhymes with) and has branches and leaves. (Answer: tree)

NURSERY RHYMES, POETRY, AND CHILDREN'S STORY BOOKS

Other activities that help your children to focus on letter sounds at the end of words are reading and reciting nursery rhymes. While you are reading and reciting nursery rhymes, overemphasize the words that rhyme by saying them louder. Additionally, you may have your child join you by repeating the two words that rhyme and direct them to say the words with you. Point to the letters that make the same sound in the words read. Purchase or check out children's books from your local library to read aloud to your child. If you are not certain of which books to check out or purchase, seek the assistance of the library's children's department personnel.

Selected Nursery Rhymes

Hot Cross Buns (Recite or Sing)
Hot cross Buns!
Hot cross Buns!
One a penny, two a penny
Hot cross buns!
If you have no daughters,
Give them to your sons.
One a penny, two a penny
Hot cross buns!

Pease Porridge Hot
Pease porridge hot, pease porridge cold,
Some like it in the pot nine days old;
Some like it hot, some like it cold,
Some like it in the pot, nine days old.

Matching Rhyming Picture Cards

Instructions: Match pictures of items or objects that rhyme.

Materials Needed: Index cards, old magazines, newspaper ads, scissors, and tape or glue.

Implementation: Cut out and glue or paste pictures of items or objects that rhyme. Shuffle the cards and place them face down on a tabletop, on the floor, or on a counter. Direct your child to find the pictures of two items that rhyme or sound the same at the end. Remove the matched cards.

Nursery Rhyme Time

Instructions: Read a nursery rhyme for your child to identify rhyming the words.

Materials Needed: A book of nursery rhymes and rhyming book stories.

Implementation: Read the nursery rhyme or story out loud. Direct your child to clap when he or she hears words that sound the same at the end. An extension for this activity is directing your child to say another word that rhymes with the words that rhymed in the book read.

Selected Nursery Rhymes

- *1, 2, Buckle My Shoe*
- *Hickory Dickory, Dock*
- *Itsy Bitsy Spider*
- *Jack and Jill*
- *Little Jack Horner*
- *Twinkle, Twinkle, Little Star*
- *A Tisket, A Tasket*
- *Baa Baa Black Sheep*
- *Eeny, Meeny, Miny, Moe*
- *Georgie Porgy*
- *Hot Cross Buns*
- *Humpty Dumpty*
- *I'm a Little Teapot*
- *Jack Be Nimble*

Suggested Rhyming Books

- Giles Andrease, *Giraffes Can't Dance*, *Down By the Cool Pool*, and others
- Nick Bland, *Bear* series of rhyming books
- Anna Dewdney, *Llama, Llama* series
- Julia Donaldson, *The Gruffalo* series
- Dr. Suess, *The Cat in the Hat*, *Hop on Pop*, and others
- Nancy Shaw, *Sheep in a Jeep* and others in the *Sheep* series

Timed Rhyming Face-Off

Instructions: Say words that rhyme within a set time.

Materials Needed: Timer or stopwatch (optional).

Implementation: Say a word or hold up the picture of an item. Set a specific amount of time and see how many words your child says that rhyme with the word said or pictured displayed.

Letter Sound Sheet Activity

Instructions: Point to a letter and direct your child to say the sound of the letter.

Materials Needed: An old sheet or plain tablecloth and a permanent magic marker.

Directions: Write the letters of the alphabet on the sheet (uppercase and lowercase).

Implementation: Begin with the letters and sounds you are currently working on with your child. Tell your child to say the sound for each letter selected. You may also say the sound first and direct your child to find the letter that is associated with the sound heard. Extend this activity by having your child say a word, find a picture, or draw a picture for the letter sound heard.

Timed Letter Sound Scavenger Hunt

Instructions: Search for pictures or words for selected letter sounds.

Materials Needed: Old magazines, newspaper ads, newspapers, scissors, and a two-minute timer.

Implementation: Select a letter and direct your child to find a word or picture that begins or ends with the sound of the letter selected. You make a chart of the number of items found during the allotted time. Create a letter Sound Notebook by gluing the words or pictures found for each letter sound presented on a page.

I Have and Can You Find Game

Instructions: Select an alphabet letter for your child to find a picture of its corresponding sound (beginning or end).

Materials Needed: A collection of pictures, downloaded images, and alphabet letters.

Implementation: Gather a collection of pictures representing corresponding letter sounds for selected alphabet letters. Select a letter and say: *I have the letter T. Can you find a picture of something that starts with the sound in the beginning?* *Note:* You may increase the level of difficulty by having them listen for the selected letter sound in the beginning, middle, and end.

Alphabet Sound Cups

Instructions: Collect small items (trinkets) associated with alphabet letters and their sounds.

Materials Needed: Small plastic or paper cups, items from discount stores, alphabet letters (commercial or handmade), glue or paste, and a marker.

Implementation: Write or glue selected letters on the cups. Place your collection of items before your child. Direct your child to select an item, say the name of the item he or she selected, and place the item in the letter cup that corresponds with the letter's sound. Add cups as letters and their corresponding sounds are taught and learned. This is excellent for reviewing and practicing.

Erase the Sound

Instructions: Draw a picture on a dry-erase board.

Materials Needed: Dry-erase board, and dry eraser.

Implementation: Draw a picture on the board. Direct your child to find and erase the item that begins or ends with the sound of the letter you select. *Note:* You may tape pictures on the board or place pictures in front of your child. Hold up the letter and direct your child to circle or underline the item in the picture that begins or ends with the sound of the letter chosen. See example (snowman, hat, sun, book, ball, and pot) on an the dry-erase board.

Mystery Letter Bag

Instructions: Place three objects in a paper bag beginning with the same letter sound.

Materials Needed: A paper bag and selected items of your choice. For example, button, bell, and boat.

Implementation: Direct your child to remove and say the name of the items. Ask your child to say the name of or point to the mystery letter that makes the sound heard.

Guess the Letter (Ages Four to Five)

Instructions: Say three words with the same beginning, middle, or ending sound.

Materials Needed: Alphabet Letters and a list of sets of three words (self-selected).

Implementation: Place a set of selected alphabet letters before your child or write the letters on a sheet of paper. Say the three words and tell your child to hold up the letter or draw an *x* on the letter sound heard.

Letter Sound Match Activity

Instructions: Match selected pictures with the same beginning or ending sounds.

Materials Needed: One plain sheet of paper or cardstock (8.5 × 11 inches), index cards, paste or glue, and two sets of pictures (beginning and ending sounds) being taught/reviewed.

Implementation: Draw lines or fold the paper into thirds (nine squares) to make a gameboards.

Place the cards with the pictures face down on the game board or table (optional). Your child selects a card, turns it over, and says the name of the picture. Tell your child to find another picture that begins or ends with the same sound. Remove matched cards from the board.

Letter Sound Match Activity Game Board (Sample)

Universal board made with cardstock paper

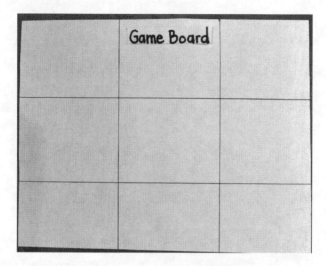

Note: This game board can be used for a variety of instructional activities and games.

Game board with pictures beginning with selected beginning letter sounds.

Pictures: wagon, lemons, flowers, tub, nose, soda, rabbit, rope, boat, and zipper

Note: Ask your child to select two pictures that begin with the same letter sound. Also, you can glue your pictures on an index card and place the picture face down on the board. Your child turns the card over, says the picture name, and finds the appropriate letter the sound picture matches. An alternate exercise activity using the same game board requires your child to place a picture or letter on the board that begins or ends with the letter sound heard. Increase the level of difficulty (ages four to five) by including listening for the letter sound in the middle of a picture or word. See the sample game board with selected alphabet letters posted.

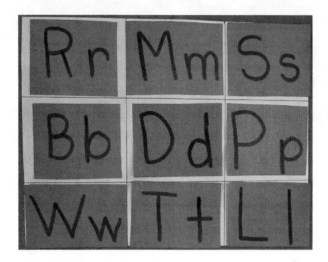

Letter Sounds Listening Game

Instructions: Say a word and your child points to the corresponding letter sound.

Materials Needed: Selected words and alphabet letters.

Implementation: Using words of your choice, say a word twice. Tell your child to point to the appropriate letter (applicable for the game board) or hold up the appropriate letter cards (commercial or homemade).

Segmented Sounds Listening Activity

Instructions: Pronounce (say) words in their distinct segments/parts.

Materials Needed: None.

Implementation: Choose a room in the house to do this activity. *Note:* The bedroom is being used as an example. Before the activity select objects in the room and your child's bedroom and divide them into sounding parts. For example, lamp (l-amp). Say the sounds *l* (l letter sound), and *amp* (short *a* sound with *mp*) twice. Direct your child to tell you the word you said. Continue using this procedure and sound out objects/items in your child's bedroom.

Sound Clapping Game

Instructions: Pronounce words that have one and two syllables (one or two parts) when spoken.

Materials Needed: None. *Note:* You may use the list of words provided to get started.

Implementation: Select one- and two-syllable words to say aloud. Direct your child to listen for the number of parts he or she hears. Say: *I will say a word twice. Listen for how many parts (syllables) you hear when I say the word. If you hear one part, clap one time. If you hear two parts, clap two times. Note:* Check to make sure your child understands what he or she is supposed to do. Provide additional practice time, if needed. Extend by adding three-syllable words.

Sample Word List

1. window (win dow)
2. walk
3. table (ta ble)
4. rainbow (rain bow)
5. trunk
6. carton (car ton)
7. runner (run ner)
8. scrape
9. washcloth (wash cloth)
10. wave
11. tub
12. maple (ma ple)

Syllabication Listening Picture Cards (Word Parts)

Instructions: Select the number that indicates the number of syllables heard.

Materials Needed: Pictures of objects with one or two syllables, one pack of 3-×-5-inch index cards, glue or tape, scissors, clothespins, and a black marker.

Implementation: Tape or glue one picture on a card and write the number one (1) and two (2) on the righthand corner of the card. Direct your child to say the name of the picture and clip the clothespin on the number that tells him or her how many syllables (word parts) are heard. *Note:* Children may circle, underline, or circle the number heard. See the example pictured.

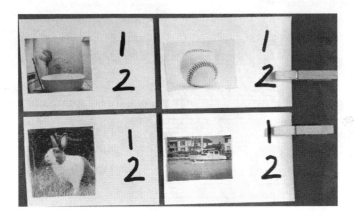

Syllabication Listening Picture Cards Example

Pictures: Tub, Baseball, Rabbit, and Boat
Syllabication Pictures or Words Hunt

Instructions: Find pictures of items or words with one or two syllables (word parts).

Materials Needed: Old magazines, newspaper ads, scissors, and a tablet or notebook (optional).

Implementation: Direct your child to find and cut out pictures/images or words that have one or two syllables (word parts). *Optional:* Your child may make his or her own notebook of pictures and words with one or two syllables. Also, you may increase the level of difficulty by having him or her find pictures for three-syllable items or words.

What Word Did I Say?

Instructions: Pronounce syllables (word parts) or the individual sounds of selected one, two, and three-syllable words.

Materials Needed: A collection of one, two, and three-syllable words to pronounce.

Implementation: Say each word to your child in syllables (word parts). Direct your child to tell you the word you said. For example, say: *I am going to say some sounds. I want you to put the sounds together you hear and tell me the word I am saying.* Say: *d-o-g, Yes, dog is correct.*

Note: You may select words used in the Sound Clapping Game.

The activities presented in this chapter are designed to introduce parents and caregivers and their children to phonemic awareness, a very necessary component of reading. Utilize as many of the activities as possible. Do not be overly concerned if you need to spend more time than you anticipated in this section. Developing and strengthening the ability to hear distinct sounds of letters in words will assist children in unlocking unknown words or vocabulary throughout their educational journey.

CHAPTER 4 SUMMARY

Phonological awareness and phonemic awareness skills are essential for the process of learning to read. These skills center on children's ability to hear and distinguish sounds of letters, syllables, words with the same beginning sounds, and rhyming words. The first layer of the foundation for this reading plan starts with recognition and discrimination of the alphabet letters. The parents and caregivers are guided through letter recognition and letter discrimination through instructional activities and games. Also, recommended ways to present the letters to children are provided for parents and caregivers to consider or utilize.

Additionally, the instructional activities provided include specific instructions, materials needed, if applicable, and steps or directions for implementing the games and instructional activities at home. There are selected instructional games with *scripted* lessons to assist parents and caregivers in presenting the lesson to their children. The author encourages parents and caregivers to spend additional time on sections or areas where children's performances indicate additional practice is needed. Parents and caregivers can utilize word lists and other pertinent listings of songs, books, and nursery rhymes cited in the resource book.

Along with teaching children the sounds of individual alphabet letters, parents and caregivers are also providing instruction to develop children's ability to listen to ending letter sounds, rhyming words, and syllables (one-, two-, and three-word parts). The upcoming section of the raising readers plan, chapter 5, is continuing to work with letters and sounds with a focus on the blending of letter sounds (consonants and digraphs) and vowels. Another significant prereading skill layer is being laid to assist you in building a strong foundation for the learning-to-read process.

Chapter Five

Putting It Together

Auditory Blending of Letters, Vowels, Consonants, and Digraphs

This chapter focuses on the auditory blending of letters, vowels, consonants, and digraphs. If this is where you are starting in the raising readers at home plan, it is assumed your child has mastered the alphabet letters (uppercase and lowercase) and has a sound footing with their individual sounds (phonemes). Also, they are familiar with rhyming words and syllables (word parts). Children who have not demonstrated understanding and knowledge in the aforementioned areas should review a prior chapter related to their area of need.

Children who began in chapter 2 and have completed chapters 3 and 4 should be ready for additional work with letter sounds (blending), vowels, consonants, and digraphs. Chapter 5 adds another layer to the reading foundation to support and strengthen the reading process in the home. Instructional activities and games presented are designed to further develop the auditory blending of letter sounds and provide additional practice. Parents and caregivers will learn how to introduce their children to vowel letters/sounds, consonant clusters (blends), and digraphs. Additionally, children are introduced to a skill needed as future readers—unlocking words.

All readers must learn how to break words into their distinct parts by letter sounds. This skill enables them to unlock unfamiliar and new words as they proceed through their reading journey. As children become more knowledgeable and skillful in letter sounds and word parts, they develop a toolbox of strategies to pronounce and acquire new reading vocabulary. This section will begin with a brief explanation of what consonant blends, vowels, and digraphs are. It is important and necessary for parents and caregivers to use the information shared to find items in their home environment that can serve as examples and models for these new letters and sounds.

Seeing examples in their home environment will help children relate to new sounds learned with more meaning. After gaining a clearer understanding of consonant blends, vowels, and digraphs, parents and caregivers should spend time finding appropriate items in their homes to cement new learnings. Every effort should be made to provide opportunities for children to practice with objects they are familiar with in their homes. For example, a clock (*cl*) is an ordinary item found in homes that serves as a model for the consonant cluster *cl*.

WHAT ARE CONSONANT CLUSTERS (BLENDS)?

Consonant clusters (blends) are two or three letters that appear together at the beginning *or* end of a word. Each letter makes its own distinct sound. When the two or three sounds are blended (spoken together), each individual letter's sounds are heard and make up the word. For example, in the word string, *s*, *t*, *r* are heard when the word is pronounced.

List of Selected Consonant Blends with Key Words

- *sk skunk*
- *st stop*
- *gl globe*
- *cr crate*
- *gr great*
- *pl plow*
- *str strip*
- *spr spring*
- *spl splash*
- *ng ring (end)*
- *nt cent (end)*
- *nd hand (end)*
- *mp lamp (end)*
- *rm arm (end)*
- *rk fork (end)*

Note: This list is not all-inclusive.

WHAT ARE VOWELS?

The letters *a*, *e*, *i*, and *o* are called vowels. Each vowel letter has a short and long sound. The letter *y*, however, is a consonant and a vowel. The letter *y* is considered a vowel when it is the only vowel in a word such as *gym*, *myth*, and *style*. Also, *y* is considered a vowel at the end of a word/syllable (*candy*, *deny*, *fancy*), or in the middle of a syllable (*system*, *lye*, and *type*). Children must learn the vowel sounds since they are present in all words. When vowels are produced, there is no restriction on the passage of air from the lungs to the mouth. Air is restricted by either the throat, tongue, lips, or teeth when producing consonants.

Long vowels are easier to learn because the sounds of the long vowels match the names of the letters—*a*, *e*, *i*, *o*, and *u*. Also, children must learn vowel sounds since they are present in all words in the English language. The author of this plan chose not to include the long vowel and silent *e* (*mat-mate*), vowel teams such as *ai* in *wait*, *ea* in *meat*, *oa* in *boat*. This decision, however, does not prevent parents and caregivers from introducing other vowels or letters. Children will, however, receive more in-depth formal phonics instruction beginning in kindergarten or homeschool educational setting.

List of Words Representing Vowels (Short and Long) with Selected Key Words

Short Vowel Words

- *cat "a"*
- *pet "e"*
- *pin "i"*
- *log "o"*
- *nut "u"*
- *myth "y"* (y sounds like "i" in pin)

Long Vowel Words

- *cake "/a/"*
- *feet "/e/"*
- *kite "/i/"*
- *go "/o/"*
- *cute "/u/"*

Note: This list is not all-inclusive. Other vowel letter combinations representing long sounds are not included in this plan.

WHAT ARE DIGRAPHS?

Consonant digraphs consist of a combination of letters that produce a single sound. You do not hear the distinct sound of each letter in the consonant combination such as *sphere*, *when*, and *phone*. The two letters represent one sound. Children must learn and know what digraphs are and that they make *one* sound to enable them to read unknown and new words. Common digraphs are: *ch* (church), *ch* (school), *ng* (king), *ph* (graph), *sh* (shoe), *th* (then), and *wh* (what). Parents and caregivers can explain a digraph to children by describing them as best friends working together to make one sound.

The brief discussion shared was designed to give readers a short introductory review of consonant blends, vowels, and digraphs. Parents and caregivers are encouraged to seek additional information if interested in expanding and extending beyond what the author included. The upcoming instructional activities and games are centered on the basic information needed for this layer of the reading foundation plan. The author is aware that children progress differently and strongly recommends that parents and caregivers provide adjustments necessary to address individual skill needs. This section begins with auditory consonant blends and vowels (short and long).

The following instructional activities and games begin by providing brief exercises to guide children toward listening for consonant blends at the beginning of words. It is recommended that parents and caregivers start with single initial consonant sounds first and then move into listening for two or three consonant letter sounds at the beginning and the end next. Also, vowels (short and long) will be incorporated before digraphs. Adding vowel sounds along with consonant blends will introduce children to words they'll be able to sound out and read. Additionally, readers always have the option to change the order to meet individual skill needs.

AUDITORY CONSONANT SOUND BLENDING REVIEW

Instructions: Say each letter sound (phoneme) of words.

Materials Needed: None.

Implementation: Using a list of words with the consonant, vowel, consonant (CVC) pattern such as cat (c-a-t), pronounce each letter sound (phoneme). Direct your child to say the word he or she hears. Continue with your list of words. Determine how long you want to continue this review. *Note:* As an option, display pictures/images representing your selected words and tell your child to point to the picture that shows the word sounded out.

Suggested List of Consonant, Vowel, Consonant Words

- sat
- pen
- net
- cap
- jam
- man
- bed
- rag
- hen
- dog

Consonant Blend Scavenger Hunt

Instructions: Pronounce the consonant blend sound and the child searches for the picture.

Materials Needed: Pictures from old magazines, downloaded images, or objects.

Implementation: Say: *I am going to say a word that has two letter sounds you will hear in the beginning. Listen carefully for the first two sounds you hear. Say the sound of the two letters twice in seconds.* Direct your child to name the two letters he or she hears at the beginning of the word. Then instruct your child to find the picture or objective that begins with the two letters he or she hears. *Note:* This activity can be held inside or outside.

Consonant Blend Picture Cards

Instructions: Match pictures with selected consonant blends.

Materials Needed: Game board, cardstock, index cards, pictures, glue, and scissors.

Implementation: Pronounce a word representing selected beginning consonant blends. Direct your child to find pictures of items that have the same beginning consonant as the word you said.

Note: Pictures may be glued to index cards or a game board may be created using cardstock.

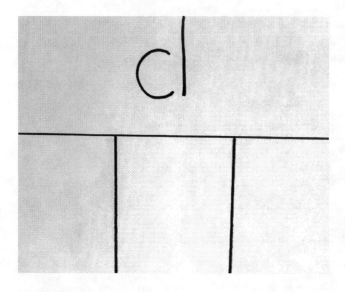

Completed Sample Game Board

Pictures: clap, clips, and clown

Note: An alternate activity is directing your child to draw a picture of something that begins with the consonant blend *cl.*

Consonant Blends Words Search

Instructions: Find words that begin with selected consonant blends.

Materials Needed: One pack of index cards (4 × 6 inches), black marker, cardstock (8.5 × 11 inches), old magazine or newspaper ads, and scissors.

Implementation: Cut the index cards in half and write your selected consonant blends on the index. Place the cards across the top row of the chart. Direct your child to find words that have the consonant blends posted on the chart. *Optional:* Collect the words found and place them in a Consonant Blends Notebook for future use.

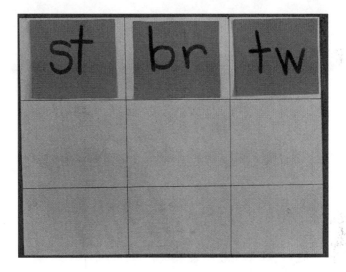

Which Consonant Blend Am I?

Instructions: Name the beginning consonant blend heard.

Materials Needed: A collection of objects or items representing selected consonant blends and a paper bag.

Implementations: Place your selected objects or items in a bag. Direct your child to select an item and say the name of the item and the beginning blend (two letters) heard. *Optional:* Children may find another object in a room that begins with the same blend or say a word.

Roll with Consonant Blends (Beginning and End)

Instructions: Blend beginning consonant clusters with word ends.

Materials Needed: Clothespins, empty paper towel, black marker, index cards, scissors, and glue or tape.

Implementation: Cut an empty paper towel holder in half through the middle. On the right end of the roll, write the selected word ending with a black marker. Write a consonant blend on an index card and tape the card on the front side of the clothespin. Say the consonant blend and ending word part. Direct your child to put the sounds together and tell you the word.

Sample Instructional Activity—Roll with Consonant Blends

St Consonant Blend or Cluster

Stop

Stick

Stem

Additional Practice Exercises

Instructions: Pronounce the consonant blend and word part.

Materials Needed: One sheet of 8.5 × 11 inch-cardstock, scissors, and a black marker.

Implementation: Pronounce the selected consonant blend and word part. Direct your child to say the word you are pronouncing. *Note:* Children may be directed to find pictures or images that represent consonant blended pictured in the example (*cl*) blend.

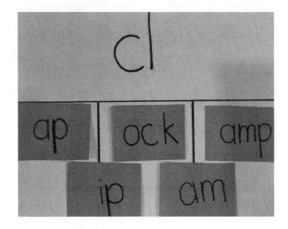

Clap, Clock, Clamp, Clip, and Clam

Bend, Find, and Band

LONG AND SHORT VOWELS

This section provides instructional games and practice exercises with long and short vowels. It is permissible to work with the long and short vowels while providing instruction on consonant blends. The author recommends that you work with them together after your child has demonstrated an understanding of the consonant blends. Monitor and assess your child's readiness. If your child experiences any difficulty, spend more time on strengthening the area needed before moving on or adding additional concepts or skills. Always begin each new concept or skill with what is familiar to children in their home environment.

Learning vowels can pose a challenge to children. One of the main challenges to learning vowels is that they are not *felt* in the mouth. Children can feel the friction with their tongue, lips, or teeth when producing consonant sounds. Next is the difficulty distinguishing between short and long vowels and similar vowel sounds. Also, for the long vowel sound to be heard, you add the silent *e* such as *hat* to *hate*. Or two vowels together can result in producing a long sound of the vowel such as *ea* together in the word *beneath*.

It is recommended, however, to start teaching the short vowels first because there is a wealth of CVC words young children are exposed to or come across during their early reading. Although it may be a little harder for children to remember the sounds of the short vowels, they will experience success with practice and support. Parents and caregivers should review the short sounds of the vowels before beginning instruction with their children. There is a wealth of YouTube tutorial videos as well as websites on vowel sounds for review and practice.

Exactly when is your child ready to learn vowel sounds? Your child is ready to learn vowels when he or she can hear vowel sounds in simple CVC words. The following is a list of words and brief instructions parents and caregivers can use to determine if their children can hear vowels in simple three-letter CVC words when pronounced. *Note:* A short list of suggested short CVC words is provided for optional use. Parents and caregivers may create their own list of words to use with their children.

Listening for the Short *A* Vowel Sound

Instructions: Read aloud one-syllable words with the short *a* sound.

Materials Needed: A selected list of CVC words and a picture representing the short *a* sound such as cat.

Implementation: Say: *Today you are going to listen for the short* a *sound.* Point to or hold up the picture of the cat. Say: *This is a picture of a cat. Say the name of the picture with me: cat.* Repeat and pronounce each phoneme (c, a, t). Say: *The sound you hear in the middle is the short* a. Say the short *a* sound aloud again. Say: *I am going to read a list of words. Raise your* a *when you hear the short* a *sound when I say the word.*

A Suggested List of Short CVC Words

- top
- mat
- wet
- tip
- dad
- bin
- cut
- cap
- bad
- fog
- bat
- get

It is recommended to start teaching the short vowels first because there is a wealth of CVC words young children are exposed to or come across during their early reading. Although it may be a little harder for children to remember the sounds of the short vowels, they will experience success with practice and support. Parents and caregivers should review the short sounds of the vowels before beginning instruction with their children. There is a wealth of YouTube tutorial videos as well as websites on vowel sounds for review and practice. The following is a list of short vowel sound words (examples) for additional auditory listening.

Short A

- cap
- bat
- bad
- cat
- dad
- lap
- tap
- map

- pat
- nap

Short E

- bed
- get
- pen
- bet
- wet
- fed
- net
- ten
- hen
- met

Short I

- bin
- tin
- sip
- tip
- pin
- zip
- did
- win
- nip
- wit

Short U

- bun
- cut
- pup
- cup
- sun
- sum
- run
- fun
- rug
- hug

SHORT VOWEL INSTRUCTIONAL ACTIVITIES AND GAMES

Short *A* Auditory Exercise

Instructions: Read a list of select long *a* words aloud.

Materials Needed: A selected list of words with a collection of short *a* vowel words and other short vowel words and old magazines or newspaper ads.

Implementation: Say: *I am going to read words to you. I want you to listen for the short* a *sound.*

Make the short a *sound. Raise your hand when you hear short* a *sound in the word I say. Let's practice first.* Say: *Cat and the short* a *sound.* Repeat the word and short *a* sound twice. Follow this same procedure throughout this activity. Find a short *a* picture in a magazine or ad.

Short Vowel Sound of the Day

Instructions: Search for objects or objects in the house for selected vowel sounds.

Materials Needed: Items or objects representing short *o* and a timer (optional).

Implementation: Say: *Today, we are going to find items or objects in the house that have the short* o *sound. What sound does the short* o *make? Let's see what items you can find in three minutes. Note:* Parents and caregivers may strategically place items in a room.

Short Vowel Notebook

Instructions: Collect pictures of items for *a, e, i, o,* and *u* vowels.

Materials Needed: Old magazines, a small notebook, newspapers, newspaper ads, downloaded images, scissors, and glue.

Implementation: Direct your child to find pictures of items that have the short sound of each vowel presented. *Note:* This activity may be extended by having children search for words that have the short vowel sound. Also, to check their understanding of the word, ask them to use the word in a sentence or tell you what the word means, if applicable.

Short Vowel Sound Search in the Environment Activity

Instructions: Point out words in the environment (signs or print) that contain short vowel sounds.

Implementation: Use traveling, grocery shopping, visits to museums, or on nature walks to focus and reinforce short vowel sounds shared and taught. Show your child signs, billboards, labels, and store advertisements with words containing short vowel sounds. Screenshot pictures of the words for later use as a review or a practice activity. *Note:* The screenshot pictures can be placed in your child's notebook or tablet.

Short Vowels Scavenger Hunt

Instructions: Hide objects representing selected short vowel sounds outside.

Materials Needed: Objects representing short vowel sounds.

Implementation: Direct your child to search for selected objects placed outside. He or she must say the short vowel sound of the object found. *Note:* This activity can also be held indoors.

Short Vowels Riddle Game

Instructions: Provide clues for riddles with short vowel words as answers.

Materials Needed: Create your riddles for each selected short vowel taught. *Note:* The author's created riddles may be used as a guide/example.

Implementation: Say: *I am going to give you clues to help you guess the answer. You will hear a short vowel sound when you say the correct answer.* Direct your child to say the name and sound of the short vowel he or she hears.

Short Vowel Sound Riddles

1. I am thinking of something that you can drink out of. What is it? (cup, glass)
2. I am thinking of a farm animal that says *oink oink*. What is it? (pig)
3. I am thinking of something used to hit a ball. What is it? (bat)
4. I am thinking of something that you write with. What is it? (pen)
5. I am thinking of that has five fingers. What is it? (hands)
6. I am thinking of something that lays eggs. What is it? (hen, chicken)

7. I am thinking of something you can use to blow cool air. (fan)
8. I am thinking of something you may cook food in. What is it? (pan, pot)
9. I am thinking of something a spider makes. What is it? (web)
10. I am thinking of something that shines in the sky. What is it? (sun)

Short and Long Vowels Water Bottle Bowling

Instructions: Children say a short word for the short or long vowel water *pin* knocked down.

Materials Needed: Ten empty water bottles, a small ball, index cards, a marker, and tape.

Implementation: On an index card, write the letter for each short and long vowel. Tape a card to each bottle. The object of the game is to knock down the pins. Direct your child to say the vowel letter sound and a word for each pin that falls. There are alternate ways to play this game. You may have your child knock down the pins that make the sound you say. Or, say a word and ask your child to knock down the pin that makes the short or long vowel sound he or she hears.

Short Vowel Water Gun Fun Activity

Instructions: Say words or display pictures representing a short vowel sound.

Materials Needed: A water squirt gun, five balloons, marker, string, and words or pictures representing each short vowel sound.

Implementation: Write the vowel letters on each balloon with a permanent marker. Blow up the balloon and tie a string around each balloon. Secure the balloons to the back of a chair outside. Direct your child to squirt the balloon that represents the vowel sound heard when you say the word or hold up a picture.

Short Vowel Index Cards Exercise

Instruction: Blending and practicing selected short vowel sounds in CVC words.

Materials Needed: Selected beginning and ending consonant sounds, short vowels, index cards (3 × 5 inches) lined or unlined, CVC words, and black marker or crayon.

Implementation: Fold over both ends of the index card. Write a beginning letter and ending letter on each folded section. In the center, write a short vowel letter. Select words that follow the CVC pattern. Direct your child to say and blend the beginning, short vowel, and ending sounds together. Provide additional assistance as needed.

Short Vowel Index Card picture

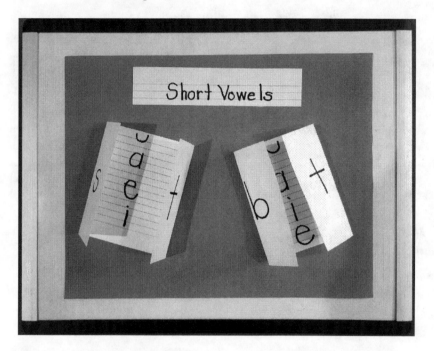

Short Vowel Sound Bean Toss Game

Instructions: Place a bean in the short vowel cup that represents the short vowel sound heard.

Materials Needed: Five plastic or paper cups, a black marker or crayon, and dried beans (lima beans or black-eyed peas). *Option:* A small ball may be used instead of the beans in this game.

Implementation: Write a short vowel letter on each cup. Say a short vowel word. Direct your child to toss or place a bean in the cup that makes the short vowel sound he or she heard. *Note:* You may use pictures instead of beans. Also, this game may be played inside the home or outdoors.

LONG VOWEL SOUNDS ACTIVITIES AND GAMES

Long Vowel Search Activity

Instructions: Find pictures of items representing each long vowel sound.

Materials Needed: A collection of pictures representing each long vowel sound, the long vowel chart, glue, and a brown paper bag.

Implementation: Place the collection of pictures in a brown paper bag. Direct your child to select a picture from the bag and say the name of the picture. After saying the name of the picture, tell your child to place the picture under the long vowel sound heard. *Note:* Children may draw their own pictures. They still need to say what they drew. The long vowel chart is pictured here.

Long *E* and Long *O* Review Exercise

Instructions: Find long *o* and long *e* items in the house.

Materials Needed: None. The game board is optional.

Implementation: Review (brief) the long *e* and long *o* vowel sounds. Direct your child to find long *o* and long *e* items in the house. *Note:* Children may also search outside.

Three Nose

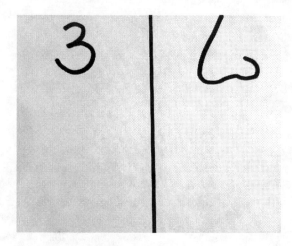

Long Vowel Popsicle Puppets

Instructions: Hold up the long vowel popsicle stick that represents the long vowel heard.

Materials Needed: Popsicle sticks, a black marker, and a selected list of long vowel words or pictures.

Implementation: Using a black marker, write a long vowel letter on each stick. Say a long vowel word or display a picture. Direct your child to show you the vowel letter sound he or she hears.

Example of Popsicle Sticks

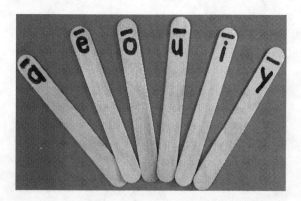

Long and Short Vowel Hand Review Activity

Instructions: Tap a finger and say a word or find a picture that represents that long/short sound.

Materials Needed: Hands template, a collection of pictures representing long and short vowel sounds. *Note:* Parents and caregivers may trace their child's hands on a sheet of cardstock paper instead of using the hand template.

Implementation: Tap your child's finger (randomly). Direct your child to say a word or point to a picture that has the vowel sound specified. The hands template and sample are next.

Hands Template

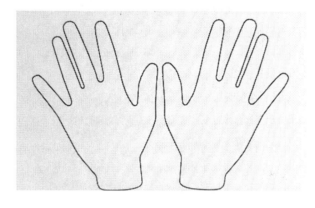

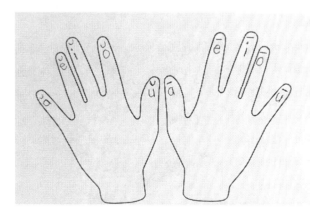

Long Vowel Sound Trail Activity

Instructions: Say a word that represents the long vowel stepped on following the trail.

Materials Needed: Five sheets of cardstock paper and a black marker.

Implementations: Using the black marker, write a long vowel sound (*a*, *e*, *i*, *o*, and *u*) on each sheet of paper. Laminate the sheets of paper for durability before use. Make a trail outside by spacing the cards two to three feet apart. Direct your child to walk down the trail and say a word or name something outside that has the vowel sound they walk on. *Note:* Extend this activity by including the long vowel sounds too.

Swatting Long Vowel Sounds

Instructions: Swat long vowel sound words when heard.

Materials Needed: Hands template, cardstock paper, two popsicle sticks, a list of long vowel and short words, and glue.

Implementation: Use the hands template or homemade hand to create the vowel swatter. Direct your child to listen to the word you say. He or she *swats* the invisible word with the vowel swatter when a long vowel sound is heard. Extend this activity by including the short vowel words. Tell your child to say the name of the vowel and hold up the long or short vowel hand.

Long and Short Vowel Words Swatter Example

Long Vowel Sound Picture Match Activity

Instructions: Match pictures with the same long vowel sounds.

Materials Needed: Pictures for each long vowel sound, index cards, and glue.

Implementation: Glue pictures on index cards. Make sure you have at least two pictures for each long vowel sound. Shuffle the cards and place them picture-side down on a counter or table. Direct your child to turn over a card, say the name of the picture, and say the long vowel sound heard. Next, tell your child to find another picture with the same long vowel sound. Extend this activity by having your child name a long vowel object or item in your home.

BEGINNING AND ENDING CONSONANT DIGRAPH EXERCISES AND INSTRUCTIONAL ACTIVITIES

Selected Sample Digraph Word Lists

CH

- bench
- chair
- chest
- charge
- charm
- check
- chick
- peach
- match

CK

- back
- jack
- wick
- truck
- lick
- deck
- flick
- crack

TH

- tooth
- cloth
- math
- that
- month
- that
- thing
- thump

SH

- brush
- fish
- shack
- shop
- swish
- trash
- wash
- shift

WH

- whip
- wheat
- whale
- which
- white
- wheel
- whine
- whisk

PH

- graph
- phase
- phobia
- trophy
- phone
- photo
- phrase
- phonics

NG

- hang
- clang
- king
- sing
- swing
- tong
- ring
- prong

QU

- quack
- quiz
- quilt
- queen
- quill
- quit
- quill
- quote

Note: These lists are not all-inclusive and are included as examples for readers.

Beginning Digraph (CH, TH, WH, SH) Instructional Activities

Instructions: Find pictures of items with selected digraph sounds at the beginning of words.

Materials Needed: Pictures of objects representing selected beginning consonant digraphs.

Implementation: Say: *We are going to review consonants that help each other and make a new sound. These consonants that work together are called digraphs. We are learning about* c *and* h. *When they are working together, a new sound is formed.* It is *ch* (say the sound). Find and place pictures of items that have the *ch* sound at the beginning of the chart. *Note:* Use the template provided or create a chart for all digraphs.

CH Digraph Template

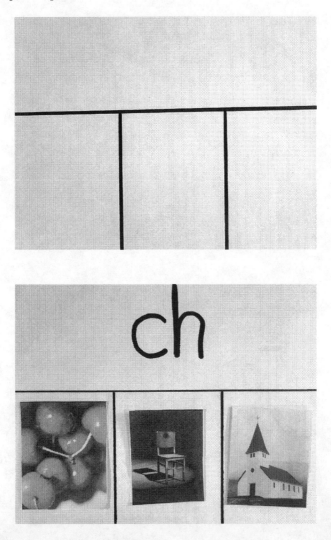

Pictured items above—cherries, chair, and church

Digraph Tic Tac Toe

Instructions: Say a word that begins or ends with a digraph.

Materials Needed: Tic Tac Toc board, digraph words or pictures, and a marker or crayon. *Note:* The Tic Tac Toe board may be drawn on an 8.5 × 11-inch sheet of paper.

Implementation: Say: *I am going to say a word or show you a picture. Listen for the digraph you hear at the beginning or end of the word/picture. Tell me the digraph sound you hear when I say the word or show you the picture.* Your child marks the Tic Tac Toe board with an *x* or *o* if he or she responds correctly.

Digraph Search

Instructions: Find items, pictures, and words with digraphs.

Materials Needed: Digraph game board (optional), old newspaper and magazines, and scissors.

Implementation: Direct your child to find words or pictures that represent each beginning and ending digraph specified. *Note:* This activity can be conducted during a walk, traveling, or shopping. Children may write the words or draw a picture of objects seen.

Digraph Search Template

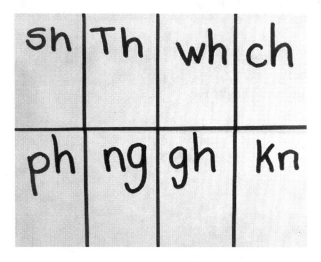

Paper Plate Digraph Activity

Instructions: Blending selected beginning digraphs with word endings.

Materials Needed: Two paper plates, a brass fastener, black magic marker or crayon, and scissors.

Implementation: See the pictured examples to create the digraph paper plate. Say: *I am going to say the sound of the* sh *digraph and the ending word part on the plate. Listen carefully and say the* sh *digraph and ending word part. Say the word you hear when the sounds are put together.* Extend this activity by directing your child to use the word in a sentence or say another word that begins with the same *sh* digraph sound.

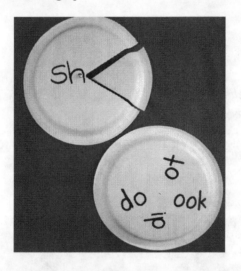

Beginning and Ending Digraph Listening Activity

Instruction: Identifying a beginning and ending digraph sound in a word spoken aloud.

Materials Needed: Selected words with digraphs at the beginning and end and two 3-×-5-inch index cards with the letter *B* written on one index card and letter *E* written on the other index card.

Implementation: Select a digraph word to say aloud to your child. Direct your child to listen for the digraph sound heard at the beginning or end of the word. Tell your child to hold up or point to *B* if he or she hears a digraph at the beginning and hold up or point to *E* if the digraph is heard at the end. Also, your child must identify the consonant digraph letters.

Digraph Match Game

Instructions: Match pictures representing digraphs at the beginning and end when spoken.

Materials Needed: Selected pictures from old magazines and newspaper ads, index cards, and tape/glue. *Note:* Images may be downloaded from the internet for pictures (optional).

Implementation: Collect a mixture of pictures representing digraphs and tape/glue each picture on an index card. Shuffle the cards and place them face down on a counter or tabletop. Direct your child to turn a card over and find another picture card that has the same consonant digraph sound (at the beginning or end) as the card he or she turned over.

Many of the templates and instructional activities presented earlier in this chapter can be adapted or adjusted to provide practice with consonant digraphs. Parents and caregivers are encouraged by the author to explore this option as they become more familiar with the different exercises and game boards. Also, readers may enlist the help of other members of the household or friends to help make game boards and gather pictures needed for selected exercises included as a part of the raising readers at home plan.

CHAPTER 5 SUMMARY

Consonant clusters, blends, vowel sounds (long/short), and consonant digraphs are essential components of phonics in helping children to move further along in the reading process. Children need to acquire a working knowledge of these word parts to enable them to unlock new and unknown words as readers. The brief review and discussions about consonant blends (clusters), vowels, and digraphs presented in this chapter provide parents and caregivers with an overview and lists of selected consonant blends, vowels, and digraphs for their information and use.

Also, the instructional activities and practice exercises in this chapter continue to emphasize and focus on auditory blending, letter sounds, and word parts. The author, however, did not include irregular vowel sounds—vowel digraphs. Parents and caregivers are encouraged to include any area not covered after determining its appropriateness for their children's level of development. The purpose of the raising readers plan is to lay a foundation that will assist children's ability to acquire prereading skills needed to become proficient readers.

By the end of chapter 5, your children should be ready to expand their acquisition of vocabulary they have already gained through this plan. Remember, as the parent and caregiver, you may revisit any chapter or section if additional practice and exposure are needed. Chapter 6 adds another layer to the reading foundation. Children will be building and exploring sight words. Learning sight words will expand children's everyday vocabulary, word knowledge, and language development.

Chapter Six

Building and Using Sight Words

Recognizing sight words is essential for early literacy and the reading process. Sight words or high-frequency words make up 75 percent of all words in children's early reading. Learning and mastering sight words eliminates or reduces the number of unknown words for children to unlock as they progress through their reading journey. Young children may get a jump start on learning and recognizing sight words that do not follow basic spelling or phonetic rules for sounding out unknown words. Children's automatic recognition of sight words enables them to experience self-confidence and success during their early stages as beginning readers.

When are children ready for acquiring sight words? How do you determine when children are ready to learn sight words? Are there basic sight words for children to learn? How many sight words should be taught in a day? These questions are addressed and discussed as another layer of the raising readers foundation is added. Recommended prerequisites to consider for learning sight words are letters or sounds knowledge, auditory blending, and knowledge of word parts or syllables. Also, other factors such as motivation, demonstrated interest in learning words, and developmental readiness levels impact the learning and acquisition of sight words.

Parents and caregivers can play an important and integral role in helping their children learn and obtain basic sight words at home. First, parents and caregivers have the unique and distinct opportunity to help their children develop and build a sight word vocabulary. Children who quickly recognize sight words are more likely to become fluent readers because they are not stopping constantly to sound out words. Also, children's reading comprehension or understanding of what they read is not hindered by starts and stops while reading. Additionally, the combination of sight words and phonics instruction increases reading speed.

Second, parents and caregivers need to determine whether their children are ready to learn sight words. Exactly, what signs or behaviors do children exhibit when ready? Children who are ready for sight word instruction will have met the necessary developmental and physical milestones (chapter 2). They will display an interest in words in books and their environment. Ready children view the pages of their favorite picture books and *read* the story aloud by themselves. Additionally, children with a genuine love for reading select books to be read aloud by their parent, caregiver, or significant others in the household.

Children learn at different rates and have different abilities. A child's specific skills, abilities, and developmental levels must be at the forefront of every parents' and caregivers' mind when planning or selecting any activity for their children. Parents and caregivers must ensure they make instructional decisions to meet their children's specific skills, abilities, and needs. Young children have short attention spans and can become frustrated easily. Therefore, parents and caregivers need to select the number of words to teach, and the amount of time to spend during instruction that aligns appropriately with their children.

Are there basic sight words for children to learn? There are lists of common basic sight words available that are used by teachers and homeschoolers as well. Two lists that are used frequently are the Dolch and Fry lists of common words. Dr. William Dolch studied and developed a list of the most frequently occurring words in children's books during his era (1930s–1940s). Dolch's list contains two hundred service words and ninety-five high-frequency nouns. Dr. Edward Fry developed a list of words in the 1950s based on the most common words appearing in reading materials for third to ninth grades. The list was updated in 1980.

Both lists are still used today and are available to parents and caregivers at no cost via the internet. Additionally, use the lists and add other words for children to learn such as days of the week, months of the year, color words, seasons of the year, and number words. The author is including a list of Dolch pre-K and kindergarten sight words for the readers' convenience. Parents and caregivers are encouraged to personalize their sight words list by adding additional words that have meaning for their child. Do not hesitate to add words when children show an interest in learning. Ensure they understand the word and always teach the word in context.

Teaching words in context means providing practice for the sight words in the everyday environment. Guide children in finding sight words in books, magazines, and newspapers. Encourage them to use the sight word as a part of their speaking vocabulary. Avoid relying totally on learning sight words through flash card drills. Flash card drills can be used, but to help promote understanding always focus on children seeing the sight words in context.

Where do you begin? Is there a select or recommended order to teach the sight words?

Experts have not developed a specific order for sight word instruction. However, there is a recommendation to begin with two- or three-letter words such as *to, his, for, is, are, the,* and *can.*

Again, parents and caregivers have the flexibility and choice to design and plan their sight work instruction to meet their children's specific needs and interests. The following selected Dolch lists are provided as starters for the readers. Parents and caregivers may use the Fry List or any other common sight word list as long as they are appropriate for a grade level-pre-K and kindergarten.

DOLCH SIGHT WORD LIST—PRE-KINDERGARTEN (FORTY WORDS)

a, and, away, big, blue, can, come, down, find, for, funny, go, help, here, I, in, is, it, jump, little, look, make, me, not, one, play, red, run, said, see, the, three, to, two, up, we, where, yellow, you

DOLCH SIGHT WORD LIST—KINDERGARTEN (FIFTY-TWO WORDS)

all, am, at, ate, be, black, brown, but, came, did, do, eat, four, get, good, have, he, into, like, must, new, no, now, on, our, out, please, pretty, ran, ride, saw, say, she, so, soon, that, there, they, this, too, under, want, was, well, went, what, white, who, will, with, yes

DOLCH SIGHT WORDS—NOUNS (NINETY-FIVE WORDS)

apple, baby, back, ball, bear, bed, bell, bird, birthday, boat, box, boy, bread, brother, cake, car, cat, chair, chicken, children, Christmas, coat, corn, cow, day, dog, doll, door, duck, egg, eye, farm, farmer, father, feet, fire, fish, floor, flower, game, garden, girl, goodbye, grass, ground, hand, head, hill, home, horse, house, kitty, leg, letter, man, men, milk, money, morning, name, nest, night, paper, party, picture, pig, rabbit, rain, ring, robin, Santa Claus, school, seed, sheep, shoe, sister, snow, song, squirrel, stick, street, sun, table, thing, time, top, toy, tree, watch, water, way, wind, window, wood

Note: The list of Dolch nouns was included for parents' and caregivers' information. There are nouns listed that young children may have learned to recognize and read because of strong exposure to environmental print.

Parents and caregivers may go beyond the grade levels included (pre-K and kindergarten) if their children are ready. The following instructional activities and games are provided to offer a variety of learning exercises and practices for children. Additionally, the author suggests and recommends that parents and caregivers include movement, singing, and sensory experiences to enhance children's sight word journey. Creating songs, chants, and stories that include the sight words taught will further cement the learning and memorization of sight words. Ten to fifteen minutes of instruction, review, or practice will help maintain their interest and motivation.

Also, incorporating using and reviewing sight words as an everyday activity where and whenever appropriate is highly recommended. Children should acquire and build their sight word vocabulary like how they acquire any other skill. They should have the opportunity to review their sight words, practice reading the sight words, and demonstrate their understanding of what the words mean in context through their language and usage.

INSTRUCTIONAL ACTIVITIES, EXERCISES, AND GAMES FOR BUILDING AND USING SIGHT WORDS

Sight Word Flash Cards

Instruction: Sight word drill, review, and maintenance.

Materials Needed: Selected sight words, index cards, and two plastic or Styrofoam cups.

Implementation: Write a selected sight word on each card. Shuffle the cards and present them at a rapid pace. Words that are identified correctly are placed in a cup labeled "Words I Know." Missed words are placed in a cup labeled "Words I Need to Learn." Keep a record of the words known and missed. The goal is to reduce the number of words not known or learned.

Sight Word Bingo Game

Instruction: Sight word recognition and memorization activity.

Materials Needed: Selected Dolch or Fry sight words taught or reviewed, Bingo game board (optional), index cards, dried lima beans, and a black marker.

Implementation: Write selected sight words previously taught on the Bingo game board. On the index cards write your selected sight words using the black marker. Shuffle your deck of sight word index cards. Say the word twice. Direct your child to cover the word you said with a lima bean. You can extend the activity by finding the sight word called in a magazine or newspaper.

Sight Word Bingo Game Board

Sight Word Search Game

Instruction: Sight word review and recognition.

Materials Needed: Old newspaper, magazine, newspaper ads, and a colored marker/pencil.

Implementation: Say: *I am going to say a sight word. Listen to the word I say and find the word I said and circle it. Let's see how many sight words you can find.*

Sight Word Match

Instructions: Sight word review and recognition.

Materials Needed: Selected sight words, index cards, and black marker or crayon.

Implementation: Write each one of your selected sight words on an index card. Briefly review the words you taught previously before you begin the activity. Shuffle the cards and place them face down on the floor, a counter, or on a tabletop. Say: *I am going to say a word. Listen carefully and point to the word I said.*

Sight Word Fishing

Instruction: Sight word recognition and review.

Materials Needed: Selected sight words, fish template, a small bowl, a card-stock/construction paper, small self-sticking magnet (circle or squares), a small stick or popsicle stick (fishing rod), and string or yarn.

Implementation: Using the fish template, trace and cut out fish for each sight word. Write a word on each fish and place a magnet on the back side of the fish. Tie the string or yarn on the end of the fishing rod and attach a magnet to the end of the string. Say: *Today you are going fishing! Let's see how many sight word fish you will catch today. To keep the fish you catch, you must say the word written on the fish. Note:* This game can be extended by directing your child to use the word in a sentence or find the word in a book, magazine, or newspaper.

Fish Template

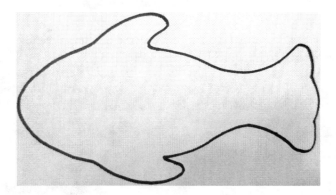

Climb the Sight Word Ladder

Instruction: Sight word review and maintenance

Materials Needed: Popsicle sticks (two different sizes), index cards, black marker/crayon, and tape.

Implementation: Write selected sight words on index cards (rungs of the ladder). Tape or glue the word to the rung of the ladder. Direct your child to read the sight word on the rung (steps of the ladder). Words correctly are placed on the ladder. Encourage your child to increase the length of the ladder by remembering the sight words learned. Ladders can be reviewed periodically for maintenance. An example of a Sight Word Ladder is pictured here.

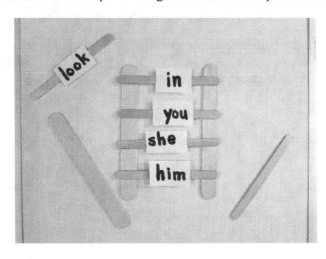

Sight Word Swiper-Dry-Erase Board

Instruction: Sight word recognition and review.

Materials Needed: Selected sight words, a small dry eraser board, a dry eraser marker, and a dry eraser.

Implementation: Write selected sight words on the board. Direct your child to erase (swipe) the word you say off the board. *Note:* Children may circle or point to the sight word.

Sight Word Eraser Board

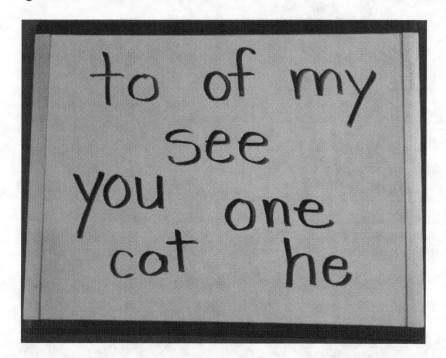

Flip the Pancakes—Sight Words

Instruction: Sight words review, memorization, and maintenance.

Materials Needed: Selected sight words, circles (size optional), marker/crayon, construction paper or cardstock, spatula (plastic), and scissors.

Implementation: Cut out the number of pancakes (circles) needed for your sight words. Write a sight word on each pancake. Shuffle the pancakes and place them with the word facing down on a table or countertop. Direct your child to flip the pancake over with the spatula and say the word written on the pancake.

An alternate activity exercise for Flip the Pancakes: Tell your child you are going to hide a pancake in one of the rooms every day. They must find the pancake sight words, pronounce the word, and find the word in a book, magazine, or newspaper. Also, your child may tape the pancake found on the door of the refrigerator or his or her bed headboard. Children can review and say the posted sight words daily. Additionally, encourage your child to use the word in a sentence. Do not hesitate to help your child form a sentence if it is needed. Always check to ensure they understand what the word means in context.

Sight Word Musical Chairs

Instruction: Sight word review and maintenance for difficult words.

Materials Needed: Select Sight words hard to remember, index cards, and a folding or plastic chair.

Implementation: Write the sight words your child is having trouble memorizing on an index card. This activity is designed to provide another fun way to study sight words. Play this game like musical chairs. Tape a sight word on the back of each chair. *Note:* Do not remove the chair when the music stops. Say: *I am going to play a game with you. Walk around the chairs and when the music stops sit in one of the chairs.* Instruct your child to say the word on the chair.

Pop the Balloons

Instruction: Sight words memorization, maintenance, and review.

Materials Needed: Selected sight words, balloons, string, a pin, and a black marker.

Implementation: Write each of your selected sight words on a balloon using a permanent marker.

After blowing up the balloons, tie the balloons to the back of a chair. Say: *I am going to say a word. Listen to the word I say. Find the word I said and pop the balloon.*

Sight Word Riddles

Instruction: Create riddles for selected sight words.

Materials Needed: Selected sight words.

Implementation: Create appropriate riddles to reinforce and review selected sight words. Direct your child to listen carefully to the riddle you say. Direct your child to say the sight word that answers the riddle. See the same riddles provided.

Sample Sight Word Riddles

1. I am an animal that says *moo*! What am I? (cow)
2. I hop and have two long ears. What animal am I? (rabbit)
3. I am an animal and I say *meow*! What animal am I? (cat)
4. I am a toy and you can bounce me up and down. What toy am I? (ball)
5. I am the color of the sky. What color am I? (blue)

Sight Word Scavenger Hunt

Instruction: Sight words review, maintenance, and recognition.

Materials Needed: Selected sight words and index cards or cardstock paper.

Implementation: Write your selected sight words on index cards or cardstock. Hide the words in different areas outside in your backyard. Say: *I have placed some of the sight words we have been learning on cards outside. I will say a word. I want you to find the word and bring the card with the word on it to me. Are you ready? Let's begin.*

Sight Word Hopscotch

Instruction: Sight Word recognition, review, and memorization.

Materials Needed: Selected sight words and washable sidewalk chalk.

Implementation: Create the outline for hopscotch with chalk on your sidewalk. In each square write a sight word. Guide your child through the hopscotch and direct them to say the word when they hop into the box. This activity incorporates movement and physical activity with learning or reviewing the sight words.

Sight Word Sentence Completion Activity

Instruction: Sight word review and maintenance with sentences.

Materials Needed: Selected sight words, index cards, and a marker or crayon.

Implementation: Create sentences for your child to complete with a correct sight word. Write a sight word on each index card and place the cards on a tabletop or counter. Read the beginning of the sentence out loud. Direct your child to complete the sentence by pointing to and saying the word that completes the sentence. Extend the activity by directing your child to say other sight words that can complete the sentence. Sample sight word completion sentences are provided.

Completion Sight Word Sentences

1. I am a _____. (boy, girl)
2. The dog ran _____. (away)
3. My hat is _____. (little, big)
4. I can run and _____. (jump)
5. My ball is not _____. (here)

Sight Word Wall

Instruction: Sight word review, recognition, and maintenance.

Materials Needed: An old sheet or plain tablecloth and a permanent marker.

Implementation: Write sight words learned or taught on an old sheet or tablecloth. Select a word or several words a day for your child to say, find, or use in a sentence. The sheet or tablecloth may be hung on a wall or spread on the floor for short reviews or drills.

Sight Word Rings, Clips, or Mini Notebooks

Instruction: Recognizing and learning color words, days of the week, number words, and months of the year.

Materials Needed: Metal or plastic rings or mini notebooks, index cards, and pictures, if applicable.

Implementation: Using a metal or plastic ring or notebook, write the number words, color words, days of the week, and months of the year. Add images and picture representations to help your child associate an image or picture with the printed word. *Note:* Determine whether your child is interested and motivated for this activity before proceeding.

Sight Word Bracelet or Necklace

Instruction: Sight word recognition and memorization.

Materials Needed: Selected sight words, index cards, hole puncher, and string or yarn.

Implementation: Cut an index card in half and write a sight word on each half card. Punch a hole in the top center of the card. String the sight words you want your child to review and memorize. Add additional sight words to the bracelet or necklace as the words are learned. Encourage your child to use the words in his or her everyday language and speech. *Note:* The sight words may be placed on rings instead of string or yarn.

Playdough and Shaving Cream Sight Words

Instructions: Sight word sensory experience for learning, review, and memorization.

Materials Needed: Selected sight words, playdough, shaving cream, and a tray/cookie sheet.

Implementation: Assist your child with forming the letters of each selected sight word. Say the name of each letter and the word upon completion. When using the shaving cream, spray and spread the cream on a tray or cookie sheet. Help your child form the letters in the shaving cream with his/her finger. Direct them to say the word, say the letters, and the sight word. *Note:* Commercial or homemade playdough may be used for this activity.

Sight Word Bean Bag Toss

Instructions: Selected sight words review and maintenance.

Materials Needed: Selected sight words, sidewalk chalk, and a bean bag.

Implementation: Draw a hopscotch frame on the sidewalk. Write a sight word in each block. Tell your child to toss the bean bag in a square. Direct your child to say the sight word in the square where the bean bag lands.

CHAPTER 6 SUMMARY

Children learning and acquiring sight words place them on the path to becoming fluent and efficient readers. Chapter 6 discussed and shared the importance of learning sight words to build vocabulary and provide young children with a way to gain confidence and have success as future readers. Parents and caregivers are presented with two common widely used basic sight word lists—Dolch and Fry lists. Adding this layer to the raising reader plan widens children's world to language and vocabulary development.

Parents and caregivers have an integral part in helping to establish and promote the acquisition of vocabulary for children by helping them learn and memorize words that do not always follow spelling and phonetic rules. The knowledge and mastery of basic sight words enable children to read fluently without stopping to pronounce words that are difficult to unlock. Children have a better understanding of passages read when they recognize words that appear frequently in early reading texts.

The instructional activities, games, and exercises presented in this chapter offer a variety of practice and maintenance for parents and caregivers to use. Parents and caregivers are encouraged to ensure their children are interested and motivated to learn the basic sight words. Also, the sight words mustn't be just taught in isolation as repeated drills. Children need to learn and use sight words in context. Additionally, the author requests that parents and caregivers determine if their children are ready to learn sight words before continuing in this chapter. Children's motivation and interest impact their learning and acquisition of basic sight words.

The upcoming chapter consists of additional vocabulary-building and development activities for children. Parents and caregivers will be able to augment their children's experiences with words through word families with additional blending opportunities. It is important, however, that parent and caregivers exercise their judgment in providing this instructional area based on their children's readiness and interest. Successful and positive experiences promote a genuine love for reading and interest in unlocking words during each child's reading journey.

Chapter Seven

We Work Together

Common Word Families

Another way to build and enhance children's reading vocabulary is through word families. Exactly, what are word families and how do they help contribute to children's literacy and reading journey? Word families are groups of words that have a similar pattern. The pattern is seen and heard at the end of a word or *rime*. For example, the word family *ate* includes words *gate*, *hate*, *mate*, and *late*. All words have the same ending letters but a different initial or beginning letter sound called an *onset*. These ending letter sounds are also sometimes called chunks. Knowledge of word families helps build fluency at early levels and builds confidence and success.

Once children become familiar with and know the patterns, they will be able to read and spell over five hundred words. Common (thirty-seven) word families are: *ack, ain, ake, ale, all, ame, an, ank, ap, ash, at, aw, ay, ate, eat, ell, est, ice, ick, ide, ight, ill, in, ine, ing, ink, ip, it, ock, oke, op, ot, ore, uck, ug, ump,* and *unk. Note:* This is not an all-inclusive list. There are, however, additional lists of word families. Learning and knowing the letters in a familiar order helps children store words in their memory. Hence, this is a positive advantage of exposing and providing instruction on word families. There are, however, experts who caution against relying heavily on learning word family lists.

Despite the effectiveness of word families adding to children's vocabulary development, there are concerns associated with too much emphasis placed on word families as the main strategy for building vocabulary. The downside of focusing on word families may cause children to look at the end of words first instead of training their eyes to always look from left to right when unlocking unknown words. Proceeding to the end of the word first and then to the beginning of the word next encourages improper movement for the eyes.

Also, as they progress further, they may encounter words that end with a rhyme but follow a different phonetic or spelling rule.

Children are exposed to word families instruction beginning in kindergarten. The author is recommending that parents and caregivers introduce word families to their five- or six-year-old children. Parents and caregivers can provide instruction on word families if they determine their children are ready to learn word patterns. The key for any instruction provided is incorporating the use of the words learned in context. Children should always use the words in their language and see the word in print. Also, parents and caregivers should check their children's knowledge and understanding of all words learned.

Word families were included as a special feature for parents and caregivers to incorporate in the raising readers plan, if interested. Selected instructional exercises, games, and activities for word families are provided and recommended. Parents and caregivers are encouraged to create their own games or modify game boards and instructional activities displayed in chapters 4 and 5. These activities are also useful for providing review and reinforcement for older siblings who have difficulties as young readers in first and second grade or are developmentally delayed.

Additionally, parents and caregivers who are interested in providing instruction on word families should begin with two- and three-letter word ending parts or chunks first. If beginning letter sounds (onsets), consonant blends, vowel sounds (long/short), and digraphs have been introduced and mastered, children should experience success with changing onsets and word ending parts. Word families lists are readily available and downloadable for use at no cost. Parents and caregivers can utilize word family word lists to help them select words that meet their children's level of understanding and knowledge. Increase the levels of difficulty based on children's needs.

The following are selected sample lists of two- and three-letter word family lists for the reader's use. The lists are not all-inclusive.

at Word Family
bat, brat, cat, chat, fat, flat, gnat, mat, pat, rat, sat, slat, spat, tat, that, vat

am Word Family
cam, clam, dam, dram, gram, ham, jam, lam, ram, scam, slam, spam, swam, tram, wham, yam

an Word Family
ban, can, clan, fan, man, plan, ran, scan, tan, than, van, pan, bran,

aw Word Family
caw, claw, draw, flaw, jaw, law, paw, raw, saw, slaw, straw, thaw,

ank Word Family
bank, blank, crank, drank, flank, plank, rank, sank, shrank, spank, tank, thank, yank

ash Word Family
bash, brash, cash, clash, dash, flash, gash, lash, hash, sash, splash, thrash, trash

ick Word Family
click, flick, kick, brick, lick, nick, pick, quick, sick, slick, stick, thick, tick, trick, wick

est Word Family
best, chest, jest, nest, pest, rest, test, vest, west, zest

WORD FAMILIES INSTRUCTIONAL ACTIVITIES, GAMES, AND EXERCISES

Word Families Picture Match

Instruction: Introduction and review of selected word families.

Materials Needed: Selected pictures representing selected word family word endings, index cards, and black marker or crayon.

Implementation: Write the word family word ending being taught on an index card. Place the index card at the top of the template. Review the sound of the word ending with your child. Direct your child to find pictures of items or objects that have the *at* sound when they say the name of the picture. Make sure your child recognizes the pictures you selected before you begin.

Word Family Picture Match Board Template

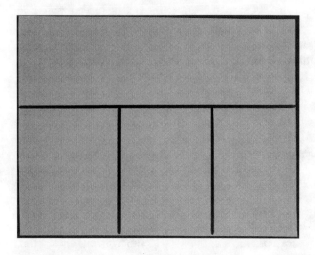

Pictured: bat, cat, and hat

Word Family Notebook

Instruction: Create a collection of word families taught for review and maintenance.

Materials Needed: Notebook or tablet, lined/unlined 8.5 × 11 inch plain paper, dividers, and black marker or pen.

Implementation: On each divider, write the word family your child is working on. As you provide instruction add the new word to the family. For example, if you are teaching the *at* word family, add each word learned—*hat, rat, bat, mat,* and *cat.* Direct your child to say the word and use the word in a sentence or find the word in a book or magazine.

Matching Onset and Word Family Exercise

Instruction: Match the beginning letter sound (onset) with the ending word part to form a word.

Materials Needed: Selected onsets, word ending parts, dry-erase board, and dry-erase board marker.

Implementation: Write selected onsets on the right side of the board (right) and rhymes on the left side of the board. Direct your child to draw a line from a selected beginning letter to an ending word part (rhyme) to form a word. After drawing the line, tell your child to say the word he or she has made. *Note:* An onset may be matched with more than one rhyme to form a word. *Optional:* Your child can be directed to find the words made in a book, newspaper, or magazine.

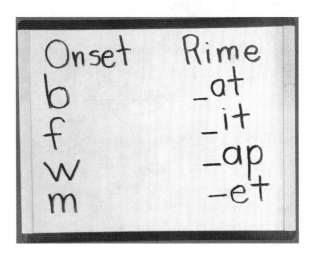

Word Families Words Ring

Instruction: Building vocabulary through word families.

Materials Needed: A ring, cards (purchased or made), index cards, a black marker, and a hole punch.

Implementation: Add words representing selected word end parts (rhymes) learned to a ring. The words may be used in sentences or reviewed periodically to maintain words learned. *Note:* Parents and caregivers determine how often to review the words acquired. Encourage children to see and use their vocabulary in context. A sample of this instructional activity is pictured here.

Word Family Hands Practice Exercise

Instruction: Recognition and auditory discrimination of selected word families words.

Materials Needed: Popsicle sticks, hand pattern/template (chapter 5), cardstock/construction paper, selected words representing word families taught, scissors, black marker, and tape/glue.

Implementation: Trace your child's hand on cardstock or construction paper for the hand pattern. Cut out a hand for each selected word family taught. Say: *I am going to say a word. Listen to the word part you hear at the end of the word. Hold up the letter sound heard at the end.*

See the Word Family Hands pictured here.

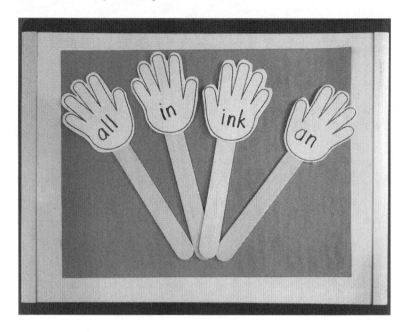

Alternate Activity for Word Family Hands

Place the hands in a brown paper bag. Direct your child to close his or her eyes and select a hand from the brown paper bag and say a word that has the same ending word part drawn.

Paper Plate Word Family Exercise

Instruction: Word Family practice, review, and maintenance.

Materials Needed: A paper plate, construction paper, brass fastener, black marker, hole punch, selected word end parts, and scissors.

Implementation: Draw lines to divide the paper plate into quarters. In each section, write a selected word part ending. Make arrows for each selected beginning sound (onset) and write it on the arrows. Punch a hole in the center of each arrow and make a hole in the paper plate with the point of the scissors. Place the brass fasteners through the arrows and paper plate.

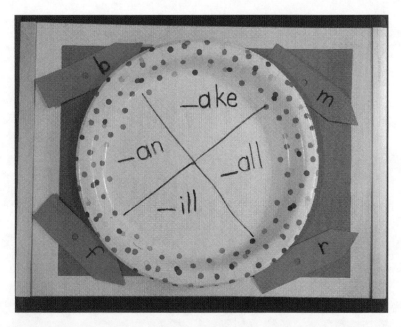

Completed Paper Plate Word Family Instructional Activity

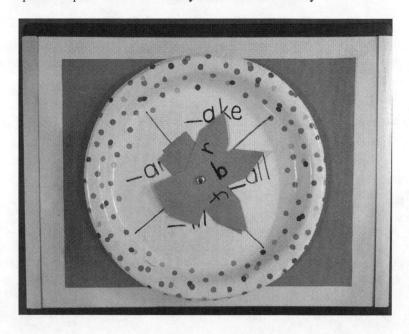

Word Family Index Cards

Instructions: Blending beginning sounds (onset) with ending word parts.

Materials Needed: One pack of index cards, a black marker, and selected onsets and word ending parts.

Implementation: Fold over one-third of the index card and write a beginning sound on the front of the folded section of the index card. On the flat part of the index card, write three word ending parts of your choice. Direct your child to blend the beginning sound with each rime and pronounce the word formed. Your child may use the word in a sentence or find the word in a book or magazine.

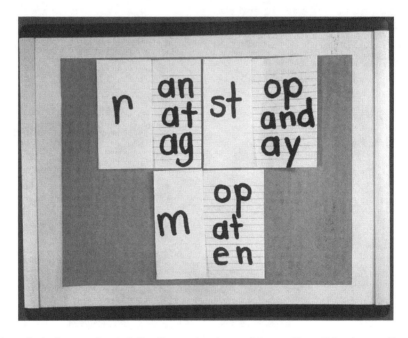

Sample index card word family cards pictured here. *Note:* Lined or unlined index cards may be used to make the word family cards.

Word Family Sentence Sense Exercise

Instruction: Word family practice and comprehension (understanding in context).

Materials Needed: Eraser board or chalkboard, eraser board marker or chalk, eraser, and pictures.

Implementation: Write sentences that need a selected word family word to complete the sentence. Read the sentence and direct your child to complete the sentence with the picture that makes sense at the end. See if your child can use the word in a sentence. Assist, if needed.

Word Families Paper Plate

Instruction: Forming vocabulary words using a variety of onsets and word ending parts.

Materials Needed: Large paper plate, brass fastener, an arrow (spinner), black marker/crayon, selected word ending parts and onsets, index cards (any size), and a brown paper bag or plastic cup.

Implementation: Divide the paper plate into sections. In each section, write selected two- or three-letter word ending parts. Make an arrow spinner out of cardstock or construction paper. Punch a hole in the center of the plate. Write onsets on index cards and place them in a bag or cup. Spin the spinner and select an onset from the bag or cup. Direct your child to say the words formed.

ALTERNATIVE ACTIVITIES FOR THE
WORD FAMILIES PAPER PLATE

Word Families Search

Instructions: Maintenance and review of word families.

Materials Needed: Old magazine or newspaper, scissors, and a timer.

Implementation: Turn the spinner to select an ending word part. Direct your child to see how many words he/she can find ending with the word ending part selected before the time runs out (two to three minutes). Have your child read the words found out loud and use the words in a sentence.

Build Words Exercise

Instruction: Make words by adding onsets to build vocabulary.

Materials Needed: A selected collection of beginning sounds (onsets) written on index cards and the word ending part paper plate.

Implementation: Shuffle the onset index cards and place them face down on a table or countertop. Direct your child to select a card, turn it over, and pronounce the beginning letter sound. Say: *Using the beginning letter sound you selected, match an onset with ending word parts on the plate to make words. Let's see how many words you make with the onset you selected.*

Hanger Word Families

Instructions: Review and maintenance of words learned.

Materials Needed: Clothes hanger, index cards, hole puncher, string, and a black marker.

Implementation: Using a clothes hanger, create a collection of words built and learned representing selected ending word parts. Label each hanger with a word ending part. Cut an index card into three parts, and punch a hole in the top center of the index card. Write the word on the card and tie the index card to the bottom section of the hanger. Use this instructional tool to review selected word family words. Children may also use the words in sentences. See the picture here.

Word Family Hanger

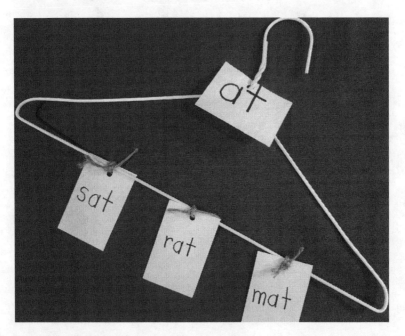

Word Family Picture Match

Instruction: Recognizing and identifying pictures representing selected word families.

Materials Needed: A collection of pictures/images representing selected word families learned.

Implementation: On the top row, place selected images representing a selected word family. Place your remaining pictures on a table or countertop. Review the pictures with your child before beginning the activity. Direct your child to select pictures that match the word family picture at the top of each row. After the chart is complete, tell your child to say the words. *Note:* Your child may search for other pictures in an old magazine or newspaper.

See the sample provided. Pictures on the top row are ham (*am*), gate (*ate*), and pail (*ail*).

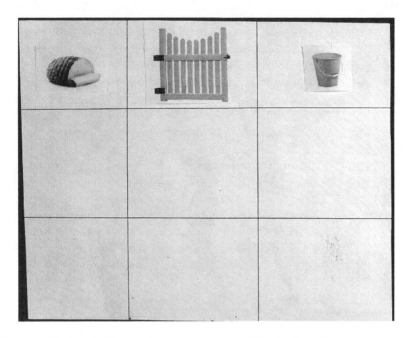

The provided activities and games are not all-inclusive. Parents and care-givers may use their own ideas, purchase commercial workbooks, or use online activities to enhance their children's exposure and experience with word families. Again, the important fact to remember is to stay tuned in to their children's interests and motivation. Learning word families is an added feature in this raising readers plan. Children who have difficulties with word families in kindergarten, first, and second grade would benefit from this section for reteaching, reinforcement, and review.

CHAPTER 7 SUMMARY

Young children develop and build their vocabulary from the time they begin making sounds and hearing language spoken around them. Learning about word families is a strategy often utilized to help develop and build vocabulary for early readers. Although many schools provide instruction on word families during kindergarten, word families are included as a special feature in the raising readers at home plan. Researchers do, however, caution educators about emphasizing the need to focus on the end of a word to unlock unfamiliar words.

Parents and caregivers are advised to ensure their children have mastered letter or sounds, consonant blends or clusters, vowel sounds, and digraphs before introducing word families. Also, it is imperative that children are motivated, have developed a love for reading, and are interested in learning more about words during their reading journey. Additionally, parents and caregivers need to provide opportunities for using the words formed in context. Learning word family words should not consist of just learning word lists. Children should be able to use the words in their everyday language, see the words in books, and demonstrate an understanding of the words learned.

Chapters 3, 4, 5, and 6 are the main layers of the raising readers plan in this resource book. Children are provided with a variety of instructional activities, games, and exercises that will enable them to have success with and confidence with word families. Since it is recommended that with older young children (five- or six-year-olds), parents and caregivers have the option of providing instruction on word families based on their children's readiness, interest, and motivation. Excluding the section on word families will not jeopardize their children's progress and reading journey. Word family instruction can be implemented when children are older.

A variety of Instructional activities, games, and exercises are provided to develop and build vocabulary. Selected word family lists (not all-inclusive) are included for reader use. Materials needed and implementations are noted for each activity and game to assist parents and caregivers in working with their children at home. Parents and caregivers play a key role in the success of the raising readers at home plan. Their consistency and support will promote and support their children's acquisition of prereading skills needed to become proficient future readers. Parents and caregivers will raise confident and successful readers at home.

Conclusion

As an elementary teacher and reading specialist, I witnessed the struggles and frustrations of children lacking knowledge of alphabet letters, letter sounds, and phonemic awareness. Children who entered kindergarten without pre-reading skills and no exposure to the print world never seemed to catch up as they progressed from one grade level to the next. Additional support through remedial reading services wasn't always successful helping them to recover and learn last year's reading skills and acquire their present grade level's reading skills and standards. Hence, a reading gap is created that follows them up through high school and into adulthood.

Learning to read is a process that all children face during the early years of formal instruction and homeschooling. Without acquiring and mastering reading by the end of third grade, children begin a path of underachievement and struggle to keep up with peers and grade-level expectations. Reading is a skill that not only affects gaining knowledge and new information but also affects an individual's future livelihood and overall well-being.

Parents and caregivers can play a major role in equipping their children with the necessary prereading skills needed to help children tackle the reading process with confidence and success. As a former educator and teacher, contributions of parents and caregivers were always welcomed, respected, and appreciated. Schools can no longer operate as islands and should reach out to enlist the assistance of their most valuable resource—parents and caregivers.

The raising readers at home plan has outlined and provided selected instructional activities, tips, and games designed to nurture and promote the development of reading skills for parents and caregivers use. Also, the plan promotes the development of a love for reading and increased parent and caregiver–child communication within the family unit. Working together as a team, parents and caregivers and schools will be able to rise to the challenge of closing existing reading gaps and producing more proficient and competent readers in the future.

Bibliography

ABC's of Literacy. "5 Pre-Reading Skills Kids Need to Be Successful." Last update: October 11, 2021. https://abcsofliteracy.com/pre-reading-skills-successful-readers/.
———. "Letter Recognition: How to Teach the ABC's." Updated March 14, 2022. https://abcsofliteracy.com/letter-recognition-how-to-teach-the-abcs/#.
———. "What Is Phonological Awareness?" Updated September 26, 2020. https://abcsofliteracy.com/phonological-awareness/#.
Arden, Melanie. "Understanding Phonemic Awareness and Phonological Awareness and How to Develop Them." *Prodigy Education*, November 8, 2021. https://www.prodigygame.com/main-en/blog/phonemic-awareness/.
Arden, Melanie. "Order to Teach Letter Recognition." Last update: March 20, 2022. https://abcsofliteracy.com/order-to-teach-letter-recognition/.
Baker, Scott, K. "The Alphabetic Principle: From Phonological Awareness to Reading Words." *National Center on Improving Literacy*. Accessed July 13, 2022. https://improvingliteracy.org/brief/alphabetic-principle-phonological-awareness-reading-words.
Brooks, Casie. "Teaching Letter-Sound Correspondence." *The Curious Hippo.com* (blog), posted August 8, 2020. https://thecurious/hippo.com/teaching-letter-sound-correspondence/.
Carcerano, Sara-Jayne. "Benefits of Reading to Your Young Children." *terra centre* (blog), posted March 17, 2020. https://terracentre.ca/blog/benefits-of-reading-to-your-baby-and-young-children/.
Cardinal, Abigail. "How to Create an Organized Home Classroom in a Limited Space." *Connections Academy*. December 8, 2020. https://www.connectionsacademy.com/support/resources/article/how-to-create-an-organized-home-classroom-in-a-limited-space/.
Celebrating Neurodiversity. "What Are Word Families and Why Are They Important to Literacy Success?" *Celebrating Neurodiversity.com*, June 27, 2021. https://celebratingneurodiversity.com/what-are-word-families-and-why-are-they-important-to-literacy-success/.

Children's Books and Reading. "Teaching Word Families." *Children's Books and Reading.* Accessed November 26, 2022. http://www.childrens-books-and-reading .com/teaching-word-families.html.

Chong, Jody. "10 Tips for Teaching Phonological Awareness." *LD@school.* Accessed September 5, 2022. https://www.ldatschool.ca/10-tips-for-teaching-phonological -awareness/.

Cox, Karen. "Learning Letter Sounds." *PreKinders.* Accessed August, 8, 2022. https://www.prekinders.com/alphabet-letter-sounds/.

Cutting, Laurie, E. "What Are the Factors That Contribute to Reading Failure?" Houghton Mifflin Harcourt Company (*hmhco.com*), (blog), posted April 11, 2017. https://hmhco.com/blog/what-are-the-factors-that-contribute-to-reading-failure#.

Flavin, Patrick. "25 Sensational Sensory Activities for Toddlers." *Rasmussen University* (education blog), posted March 7, 2022. https://www.rasmussen.edu/degrees /education/blog/sensory-activities-for-toddlers/.

Homer Blog. "Teaching Letter Sounds: 5 Fun and Easy Tips." Accessed August 18, 2022. https://www.learnwithhomer.com/homer-blog/3719/letter-sounds/.

———. "How to Teach Your Child Uppercase Letters and Lowercase Letters." Accessed August 22, 2022. https://www.learnwithhomer.com/homer-blog/6088 uppercase-letters-lowercase-letters/#.

———. "Teaching Vowels: How to Help Your Child Learn Long and Short Vowels." Accessed October 5, 2022. https://www.learnwithhomer.com/homer-blog/5814 /vowels/

———. "Reading Readiness: Top Skills for Kids to Master." Accessed March 24, 2022. https://www.learnwithhomer.com/homer-blog/3965/reading-readiness/.

Institute of Educational Sciences. "Kindergarten 2: Linking Sounds to Letters." Accessed July 29, 2022. https://ies.ed.gov/ncee/edlabs/regions/southeast/foundations /kindergarten_recommendation2.asp.

Jana, Laura, and Jennifer Shu. "Developmental Milestones of Early Literacy." *HealthyChildren.org.* Last updated June 9, 2021. https://www.healthychildren.org /English/ages-stages/baby/Pages/Developmental-Milestones-of-Early-Literacy .aspx.

Just Read. "Free Sight Words Activities You Can Use at Home." *Just Reed & Play .com* (blog). Accessed August 5, 2022. https://justreedblog.com/10-ways-parents -can-help-with-sight-word-mastery/.

Kelley, Suzanne. "Teaching Letters and Sounds: 27 Strategies That Work." *Education to the Core.* Accessed July 29, 2022. https://educationtothecore.com/2022/01 /teaching-letters-and-sounds-27-strategies-that-work/.

Learning without Tears. "Sight Words for Kids: Kindergarten and Beyond." *lwtears .com* (blog), posted September 17, 2020. https://www.lwtears.com/blog/sight -words-for-kindergarten.

———. "How to Teach Letter and Alphabet Sounds." *lwtears.com.* (blog), posted December 15, 2020. https://www.lwtears.com/blog/how-teach-letter-and-alphabet -sounds.

Light, Janice, and David Naughton. "Letter-Sound Correspondences." *Penn State University Literacy Instruction.* Accessed August 18, 2022. https://aacliteracy.psu .edu/index.php/page/show/id/6/index.html/.

Lipgloss and Crayons. "17 Ways to Practice Sight Words at Home (That Don't Involve Flashcards)." *lipglossandcrayons.com.* Accessed November 5, 2022. https:// lipglossandcrayons.com/how-to-practice-sight-words/.

Logsdon, Ann. "How to Teach a Child Early Sight Word Skills at Home." *verywell family.com.* Updated September 17, 2020. https://www.verywellfamily.com/ways -to-develop-early-sight-word-skills-at-home-2162246?print.

Lopez-Aflitto, Windy. "How to Set Up a Positive Learning Environment at Home." October 21, 2020. *Digital Promise.org.* https://digitalpromise.org2020/10/21 /how-to-set-up-a-positive-learning-environment-at-home/.

Lynch, Matthew. "Understanding Letter Recognition and Its Role in Preliteracy." *The Advocate.* November 24, 2020. https://theedadvocate.org/understanding-letter -recognition-and-its-role in preliteracy/.

Lyon, Reid, G. "Learning to Read: A Call from Research to Action." *getreadytoread .org.* November 28, 2012. https://getreadytoread.org/early-learnin-childhood -basics/early-literacy/learning-to-read-a-call-fromresearch-to-action.

Mader, Jackie. "What Parents Need to Know about the Research on How Kids Learn to Read: What Does Good Reading Instruction Look Like in a Classroom?" *hech ingerreport.org.* March 30, 2020. https://hechingerreport.org/what-parents-need -to-know-about-the-research-on-how-kids-learn-to-read/.

Mcilroy, Tanja. "15 Fun Sense of Taste Activities for Preschoolers." *Empowered Parents.* Accessed June 6, 2021. https://empoweredparents.co/sense-of-taste -activities/.

———. "21 Ways to Create a Learning Environment at Home." Accessed May 28, 2022. *Empowered Parents.* https://empoweredparents.co/learning-environment-at -home/.

———. "17 Early Literacy Skills and How to Build Them." *Empowered Parents.* Accessed June 21, 2022. https://empoweredparents.co/early-literacy-skills/.

MissKindergarten. "Teaching Reading with Word families." *MissKindergarten.com* (blog), July 24, 2022. https://misskindergarten.com/teaching-reading-with-word -families/.

Mulvahill, Elizabeth. "What Are Sight Words?" *WeAreTeachers.com.* May 9, 2022. https://www.weareteachers.com/what-are-sight-words/.

Osewalt, Ginny. "Why Are Vowels So Hard for My Child?" *Understood.org.* Accessed October 5, 2022. https://www.understood.org/en/articles/why-are-vowels -so-tricky-for-my-child-to-read-and-spell/.

Pelly, Julia. "Sensory Play: 20 Great Activities for Your Toddler or Preschooler." *healthline.com.* June 15, 2020. https://www.healthline.com/health/childrens-health /sensory-play.

PK1Kids. "Top 10 Tips for Teaching the Short Vowel Sounds to Beginning Readers and Free Short Vowel Printables." *PK1Kids.* Accessed October 5, 2022. https://pk1 kids.com/tips-for-teaching-the-short-vowel-sounds-to-beginning-readers/.

PhonoLovable Literacy. "5 Fun and Effective Ways to Teach Consonant Blends." *phonolovable.com.* Accessed October 6, 2022. https://phonolovable.com/5-fun -and-effective-ways-to-teach-consonant-blends/.

Pinola, Melanie. "How to Turn Your Home into the Best Classroom It Can Be." *New York Times.* September 15, 2020. https://www.nytimes.com/2020/09/15/realestate /how-to-turn-your-home-into-the-best-classroom-it-can-be-.html.

Power Homeschool. "How to Create a Learning-Friendly Environment in Your Home." *Power Homeschool.* September 25, 2019. https://powerhomeschool.org /articles/create-learning-environment-home/.

Raising Children Network. "Early Literacy Difficulties." *Raising Children Network.* Updated December 12, 2020. https://raisingchildren.net.au/school-age/school -learning/literacy-reading-stories/literacy-difficulties.

ReadingEggs. "5 Simple Activities to Help Kids Sound Out Words." *Reading Eggs.* Accessed October 5, 2022. https://readingeggs.com/articles/sounding-out-words-phonics/.

Reagan, Jean. "How to Make Reading Fun: 25 Ideas Kids Will Love." *Read Brightly.* Accessed March 5, 2022. https://www.readbrightly.com/how-to-make-reading-fun -25-ideas-kids-will-love/.

Reed, Deborah, K. "Effective Literacy Lesson: Teaching Consonant Digraphs." *Iowa Reading Research* (blog), posted on January 14, 2020. https://iowareading research.org/blog/effective-literacy-lesson-consonant-digraphs#.

Rice, Jenni. "Sight Words for Preschoolers." *Halsey Schools.* Accessed November 11, 2022. https://www.halseyschools.com/homefun-sight-words-for-preschoolers/#.

Richland, Katrina. "How to Teach Letters and Sounds Correctly*." Pride Reading Program.* September 6, 2021. https://pridereadingprogram.com/how-to-teach -letters-and-sounds-correctly/.

Rippel, Marie. "Top 10 Activities for Letter Knowledge." *All about Learning Press* (blog). Accessed July 29, 2022. https://blog.allaboutlearningpress.com/letter -knowledge/.

———. "Word Families: The Pros and Cons." *All about Learning Press* (blog). https://blog.allaboutlearningpress.com/word-families/.

Rock, Amanda. "Tips for Teaching Sight Words to Preschoolers." verywellfamily.com. Updated March 11, 2021. https://www.verywellfamily.com/teaching-sight-words -to-preschoolers-2764904#.

Sarah, "Teaching Letter Recognition-What Order to Introduce Letters." How Wee Learn. (blog) posted April 14, 2023. https://www.howweelearn.com/teaching -letter-recognition-what-order-to-introduce-letters/.

Scholastic Parents Staff. "4 Telltale Signs Your Preschooler Is Ready to Read." *Scholastic.* January 14, 2019. https://www.scholastic.com/parents/books-and-reading /reading-resources/language-and-literacy-milestones/get-your-preschooler-ready -to-read.html/.

Shanahan, Timothy. "Letter Names or Sounds First? You Might Be Surprised by the Answer." *Shanahan on Literacy* (blog). February 6, 2021. https://shanahan onliteracy.com/blog/letter-names-or-sounds-first-you-might-be-surprised-by-the -answer#sthash.Epm39H0V.dpbs.

————. "Time to Tell Parents the Truth about Helping Their Kids with Reading." *Reading Rockets* (blog). Commented on December 5, 2017. https://shanahan onliteracy.com/blog/letter-names-or-sounds-first-you-might-be-surprised-by-the -answer#sthash.Epm39H0V.dpbs.

————. "11 Ways Parents Can Help Their Children Read." *Reading Rockets* (blog). September 9, 2015. https://shanahanonliteracy.com/blog/letter-names-or-sounds -first-you-might-be-surprised-by-the-answer#sthash.Epm39H0V.dpbs.

Slyter, Kirsten. "14 Phenomenal Phonics Activities for Preschoolers." *Rasmussen University* (education blog). February 18, 2019. https://www.rasmussen.edu /degrees/education/blog/phonics-activities-for-preschoolers/.

Sowden, Laura. "Identifying 10 Signs of Reading Readiness." *5 Senses Literature Lessons* (blog) October 3, 2018. https://www.5sensesll.com/index.php/2018/10/03 /identifying-10-signs-of-reading-readiness/.

Tanner, Kellie. "12 Sensational Syllable Activities for Preschool." *Teaching Expertise*. March 2, 2022. https://www.teachingexpertise.com/classroom-ideas-/syllable -activities-for-preschool/.

Vivid Oranges. "Vowels for Kids: How to Identify If Your Children Are Ready to Learn Vowels?" *Vivid Oranges*. Posted November 26, 2021. https://www.vivid oranges.com/vowels-for-kids-how-to-identify-if-your-children-are-ready-to-learn -vowels/.

Watson, Susan. "20 Consonant Blends in Spelling and Sounds." *Thought Co*. Updated July 3, 2019. https://www.thoughtco.com/learning-the-blends-spelling-and -sounds-3111057.

Wright, Marissa. "What Are Sight Words?" *Teaching Expertise*. January 7, 2022. https://www.teachingexpertise.com/classroom-ideas/what-are-sight-words/.

Zettler-Greely, Cynthia, N. "Reading Milestones." *Kids Health*. Accessed March 24, 2022. https://kidshealth.org/en/parents/milestones.html/.

About the Author

Sheila E. Sapp has devoted many years to education, learning, children, and families. She has served as a classroom teacher, assistant principal, curriculum director, and elementary principal during her career as an educator. Dr. Sapp retired from the Camden County Schools System as a principal of Crooked River Elementary School, located in St. Marys, Georgia. She has an educational consulting business, Sheila E. Cares Educational Consulting and Services, LLC. Dr. Sapp is also a presenter, coach, mentor, and speaker.

Dr. Sapp is a graduate of the University of Georgia with an education doctorate in supervision and curriculum. She holds a master's in reading education (K–12) from Glassboro State College (now Rowan University) in Glassboro, New Jersey, and an education specialist degree in administration from Georgia Southern University. She has authored four books, *The Learning House*, *A Guide of Best Practices for New School Administrators*, *Staying the Course*, and *The School Connection: Parents, Teachers, School Leaders Empowering Youth for Life Success*.